The Thatcher Phenomenon

THE
THATCHER
PHENOMENON

HUGO YOUNG and ANNE SLOMAN

British Broadcasting Corporation

Published by the British Broadcasting Corporation,
35 Marylebone High Street, London W1M 4AA

First published 1986
© The contributors and the British Broadcasting Corporation 1986

ISBN 0 563 20472 9 Hardback
ISBN 0 563 20473 7 Paperback

Set in 10/12 Linotron Palatino and printed in England
by Mackays of Chatham Ltd
Cover/jacket printed by The Malvern Press Ltd

Contents

Margaret Hilda Thatcher
Biographical Details

13 Oct 1925	Born in Grantham, the daughter of Alfred and Beatrice Roberts
1936–43	Attended Kesteven and Grantham Girls' School
1943–7	Read chemistry at Somerville College, Oxford
1947–51	Research chemist
Dec 1951	Married Denis Thatcher
Aug 1953	Gave birth to twins, Carol and Mark
1954	Called to the Bar, Lincoln's Inn
1959	Elected Conservative MP for Finchley
1961–4	Joint Parliamentary Secretary, Ministry of Pensions and National Insurance
1964–6	Opposition Spokesman for Pensions
1966	Opposition Spokesman for Housing and Land
1966–7	Member of Opposition Treasury team
1967	Joined Shadow Cabinet as Shadow Minister of Fuel and Power
1968–9	Shadow Minister of Transport
1969–70	Shadow Minister of Education
June 1970	Privy Councillor
June 1970–Feb 74	Secretary of State for Education and Science
Feb 1974–Nov 74	Shadow Minister of the Environment
Nov 1974–Feb 75	Shadow Spokesman for Treasury Affairs
11 Feb 1975	Elected Leader of the Conservative party
3 May 1979	Won the General Election with a Conservative majority of 44, and became Prime Minister
9 June 1983	Won second General Election with a Conservative majority of 143

Foreword

This book is a successor to *No, Minister, But, Chancellor* by the present authors, and to *With Respect, Ambassador* by Simon Jenkins and Anne Sloman. Those three previous series of radio documentaries explored areas of Whitehall and the civil service, chronicling through the words of civil servants and ministers how British administration at home and abroad actually works in the 1980s. *The Thatcher Phenomenon* reaches into the heart of government, this time not by looking at the way the machine functions at the centre, but at the prime minister who has controlled it for the last seven years. It is emphatically not a biography, nor does it pretend to offer a comprehensive account of the Thatcher governments. Our book examines her personality, her political formation, her intellectual attitudes, and how all these have contributed to the unique style of her government. Unlike the earlier works it is entirely devoted to a politician and not a system. Like them it concerns itself not with the minutiae of policies but with the context in which policy has been made and carried out.

For the BBC this was a somewhat hazardous enterprise. It was being prepared during a period of maximum political sensitivity for the Corporation. We are especially grateful for the support of the Controller of Radio Four, David Hatch, and the Editor of News and Current Affairs, John Wilson, for trusting us to pursue the work by our usual methods, uninvigilated from above. Without this atmosphere of confidence and relaxation, it would not have been possible to make the programmes. We are equally grateful to our contributors. Mrs Thatcher's ministerial colleagues and political rivals both spoke about her with a great deal of detachment and honesty. Opposition politicians especially were willing to move outside the normal party dogfight. What the programmes presented was not only, we hope, a rounded picture of the prime minister but a more favourable picture of the minds and sensitivity of professional politicians than they often show to the world. As before, all contributors abided uncomplainingly by the stipulation we made: that they could rephrase anything during our interview with them, but afterwards they could neither change it nor have any control over how we used and edited their words.

We interviewed more than sixty contributors for the programmes, and have been able to include more material in print than was possible in the strict confines of 195 minutes' broadcasting. This means that the book covers rather more ground than the programmes. But in substance and thrust the chapters here are an unamended record of the programmes as broadcast. The only details we have changed are occasional phrases and punctuations which would not be easily intelligible if printed in their raw broadcast form. Where participants have changed their job since the early summer of 1985, when the series was broadcast, we have amended their designation accordingly. Where conversational references needed further explanation, this has been given in footnotes.

The staff of Radio Four's Special Current Affairs Programmes played a large, unseen part in the venture. We particularly thank Caralyn Jacob and Rosemary Edgerley for their unstinting assistance and support.

Hugo Young
Anne Sloman
October 1985

The Participants

Airey, Lady: widow of Airey Neave who was Opposition spokesman on Northern Ireland, 1979.

Bancroft, Lord: Head of Home Civil Service 1978–81.

Biffen, John, MP: Leader of the House of Commons 1982– .

Boyd-Carpenter, Lord: Minister of Pensions and National Insurance 1955–62; Chief Secretary to the Treasury 1962–4.

Brzezinski, Zbigniew: National Security Adviser to US President Carter 1977–81.

Castle, Barbara, MEP: Labour MP 1945–79; Minister of Transport 1965–8; Secretary of State for Employment and Productivity 1968–70; for Social Services 1974–6; MEP 1979– .

Chandler, Maurice: Oxford contemporary.

Chomacki, Dreda: Grantham contemporary.

Cooper, Sir Frank: Permanent Secretary, Ministry of Defence 1976–83.

Critchley, Julian, MP: Conservative MP 1970– .

Davignon, Viscount Etienne: a vice-president of the European Commission 1977–84.

du Cann, Sir Edward, MP: Chairman of the 1922 Committee (Conservative backbenchers) 1976–84.

Finniston, Sir Monty: Chairman of British Steel 1973–6.

Foster, John: Grantham contemporary.

Glenamara, Lord: Secretary of State for Education and Science 1968–70; Leader of the House of Commons 1974–6.

Gow, Ian, MP: Parliamentary Private Secretary to Margaret Thatcher 1979–83; Minister of Housing 1983–5; Minister of State, Treasury 1985.

Gummer, John, MP: Chairman of the Conservative party 1983–5; Minister of State, Agriculture 1985– .

Haig, Alexander: US Secretary of State 1980–2.

Harris, Lord, of High Cross: General Director, Institute of Economic Affairs 1957– .

Hattersley, Roy, MP: Secretary of State for Prices and Consumer Protection 1976–9; Opposition spokesman on Treasury and Economic Affairs and Deputy Leader of the Labour party 1983– .

9

Healey, Denis, MP: Deputy Leader of the Labour party 1980–3; Secretary of State for Defence 1964–70; Chancellor of the Exchequer 1974–9; Opposition spokesman on Foreign and Commonwealth Affairs 1980– .

Hodgkin, Professor Dorothy: Nobel prizewinner; Margaret Thatcher's chemistry tutor at Oxford.

Home, Lord: Conservative Prime Minister 1963–4; Secretary of State for Foreign and Commonwealth Affairs 1970–4.

Hoskyns, Sir John: Head of Margaret Thatcher's Policy Unit 1979–82.

Howe, Sir Geoffrey, QC, MP: Chancellor of the Exchequer 1979–83; Foreign Secretary 1983– .

Howell, David, MP: Secretary of State for Energy 1979–81; for Transport 1981–3.

Jenkins, Roy, MP: Labour MP 1948–76; Chancellor of the Exchequer 1967–70; President of the European Commission 1977–81; SDP MP 1982– .

Joseph, Sir Keith, MP: Secretary of State for Trade and Industry 1979–81; for Education and Science 1981– .

Kaufman, Gerald, MP: Opposition Home Affairs spokesman 1983– .

Kinchin-Smith, Rachel: President of the Oxford University Conservative Association prior to Margaret Thatcher.

Kinnock, Neil, MP: Leader of the Labour party 1983– .

Lewin, Lord: Chief of the Defence Staff 1979–82.

Meacher, Michael, MP: Labour spokesman on the DHSS 1984– .

Nairne, Sir Patrick: Permanent Secretary, DHSS 1975–81.

Oppenheim, Sally, MP: Conservative MP 1970– .

Parkinson, Cecil, MP: Conservative Party Chairman 1981–3; Secretary of State for Trade and Industry June–Oct 1983.

Parsons, Sir Anthony: UK Permanent Representative to the UN 1979–82; Special Adviser to Mrs Thatcher on foreign affairs 1982–3.

Patten, Christopher, MP: Director of Conservative Research Department 1974–9; Minister of State, Department of Education and Science 1985– .

Pile, Sir William: Permanent Secretary, Department of Education 1970–4.

Prentice, Reg: Labour MP 1957–77; Secretary of State for Education and Science 1974–5; Conservative MP 1977– .

Prior, James, MP: Secretary of State for Employment 1979–81; for Northern Ireland 1981–4.

Pym, Francis, MP: Secretary of State for Defence, 1979–81; Leader of the House of Commons 1981–2; Secretary of State for Foreign and Commonwealth Affairs 1982–3.

Reagan, Ronald: President of the United States 1981– .

Schmidt, Helmut: Chancellor of West Germany 1974–82.

Sherman, Sir Alfred: Director, Centre for Policy Studies 1974–84.

Shore, Peter, MP: Secretary of State for Economic Affairs 1967–9; for Trade 1974–6; for the Environment 1976–9; Opposition spokesman on Trade and Industry 1983–4; Opposition Leader of the House of Commons 1983– .

Steel, David, MP: Leader of the Liberal party 1976– .

Tebbit, Norman, MP: Secretary of State for Employment 1981–3; for Trade and Industry 1983–5; Conservative Party Chairman 1985– .

Vaughan, Dame Janet: Principal of Somerville College, Oxford 1945–67.

Walker, Peter, MP: Minister of Agriculture 1979–83; Secretary of State for Energy 1983– .

Walters, Sir Alan: Economic Adviser to Margaret Thatcher 1981–3 (part-time 1983–).

Wass, Sir Douglas: Permanent Secretary to the Treasury 1974–83.

Whitelaw, Lord: Home Secretary 1979–83; Leader of the House of Lords 1983– .

Wickstead, Margaret: Grantham and Oxford contemporary.

To the Manner Born

First Broadcast: 5 May 1985

Margaret Thatcher has given her name to the age in which we live. Whether you abominate her, as many people do, or are transfixed with admiration, that much you cannot deny her. Thatcherism is unique: not perhaps as a set of ideas, but as the only 'ism' attached to the name of a British prime minister. There were Peelites, as there were and are Heathites. Policies were Gladstonian, factions Asquithian, and a special brand of deviousness is still well described as Wilsonian. But nobody has created an 'ism' before. And nobody has more voraciously dominated a peacetime government with their personal impact and commitment than Margaret Thatcher.

Much, of course, has been written about her. But as the political leader merges, after her ten years as party leader and six as Prime Minister, into the embryonic historical personage, something more is called for: a description and assessment of the Thatcher phenomenon, not by the commentators who have perforce poured out the millions of instant words, nor by the sycophants who have been responsible for most of the biographies, but from the first-hand witnesses who have seen her at close quarters at any point in the last fifty years. Later we will be examining who she has listened to – and assessing her economic policy, her foreign policy, her social attitudes. We begin by exploring where these attitudes have come from: the experiences which formed her, the person that they created. For in one respect she is, at least in the eyes of people who have contributed to these programmes, unique. This is in the role of self. The critical link between Margaret Thatcher's conduct and her personality, remarkably unvarnished and unmoderated by the events which are sent to try her, is identified by Sir William Pile, who worked for her as Permanent Secretary at the Department of Education and Science from 1970–4:

Pile:

Everything she did, and that included all her public policies and her private discussions of those policies, sprang not from her intellect, nor were they inherited from a manifesto of somebody else's intellect, but from her own character. I've known no minister whose policies were the man to the same extent. Everything she did, all her preferences, all her prejudices, sprang from innate preferences and prejudices and the character of her upbringing and her genetic endowment. I found her a very remarkable woman who gave rise to very remarkable actions and policies as a consequence. I remember her once saying that when she was fifteen she realised there was nothing she couldn't get out of life and her only problem was to decide what it was she wanted. This was, I think, a very revealing remark and incidentally it came from somebody whose other remarkable feature is that she's got nearly everything she ever set out to get. In terms of the things she actually wanted she's had almost an unbroken track record of success. There are one or two things that are still pending as of today, but looking back over her history it is a remarkable one of having achieved what she set out to get.

In her way, she lived and breathed politics from the start, every bit as single-mindedly as any offspring of a Tory country-house grandee brought up to believe that he was born to rule. Her father, Alfred Roberts, was a shopkeeper and a Grantham politician. 'Mr Roberts,' said the report her school sent to Oxford in 1943, 'who is a local tradesman and a governor of this school, has a family of two girls for whom he has done his utmost in preparing them for careers. I have every confidence in recommending her to your consideration as I feel quite sure her family will make every effort to ensure her future success.' So this is not a rags-to-riches story but one which seems to have begun as it meant to go on. Dreda Chomacki, who still lives in Grantham, was brought up fifty yards away from the Roberts' corner shop, and has known her since primary-school days. Was Margaret Roberts a serious person even then?

Chomacki:

Quite a serious girl, yes. Not so serious that she didn't play with other children, because I remember games like hide and seek, but I think she was more serious than most children of that age. At the secondary school, I always remember her bulging satchel; it would never close, and mine never seemed to have anything in it. But I wouldn't think she had a deprived childhood, I remember parties that I went to at the shop.

The school was the Kesteven and Grantham Girls' School. Margaret Wickstead, another contemporary, also recalls a serious girl:

Wickstead:

I think I can first remember her at a lecture we had, when she must have been in the fourth year. The well-known author and lecturer Bernard Newman came to talk about spies, and gave a very amusing lecture. At the end he asked for questions in the usual way and instead of a sixth-former standing up, this young, bright-eyed, fair-haired girl from the fourth year stood up and asked him a question. But the thing that rather annoyed her contemporaries was that she asked him these questions in almost parliamentary language: 'Does the speaker think so and so?'

This air of superiority which annoyed her school friends at the time stayed with her. Margaret Wickstead recalls an occasion many years later which produced the same effect:

Wickstead:

On one notorious occasion when she was a young Member of Parliament she came back to be the chief speaker at a dinner for the Old Girls, and corrected the headmistress, who was a classical scholar, on the pronunciation of her Latin. And that very small thing turned the entire dinner party away from her. It was a very silly thing to do, actually. I don't think she'd do such a thing now.

Looking back, with the benefit of hindsight, Dreda Chomacki found little early evidence of Margaret Roberts' potential:

Chomacki:

Strangely enough, looking in old school magazines, rarely can I find any reference to Margaret. She obviously must have been quite prominent, but it's hard to find any records of her work, really. I've often looked back and thought, surely I would find Margaret's name, but not very often.

Her achievements were, as Margaret Wickstead remembers them, not untypical of any other earnest schoolgirl:

Wickstead:

She was a very good member of the school choir. She was a first class centre-half in the hockey team later on when she was in the fifth year, a hockey team which won all its matches and which stuck together with a great team spirit, which we still remember from those days.

And there was one other activity which stood her in good stead later in her career – improving her elocution. What Margaret Wickstead describes as 'a perfectly straightforward accent' was, as Dreda Chomacki remembers, perfected by learning:

Chomacki:
We had an elocution teacher at school, and several girls did do
that as a sort of extra-curricular activity, but Margaret wasn't
alone by any means in that. I can remember I had a cousin who
also did it. In fact, often I think they speak in very much the
same way, and when I hear Margaret speaking I can hear my
cousin speaking. But we also did elocution as a general part of
the curriculum: talking, poetry reading.

The Roberts' shop was a grocer's shop – fount and origin of many
an economic lecture in later years. John Foster, another
Grantham contemporary, remembers it as a thriving concern:

Foster:
They weren't wealthy, by any means, but Mr Roberts had a
very successful business. It's not the sort of business that
would be successful these days with supermarkets, but in
those days before the war it was a well-known grocer's shop in
the town, and a sub-post office as well. They lived adequately
but certainly not extravagantly.

It wasn't, as Margaret Wickstead observes, quite the scene of
poverty and struggle which legend has depicted:

Wickstead:
I think this very poor background has been overdone. I think
they were frugal, quite different. But I do think most of Margaret's school life was spent with a father who was an eminent
citizen of Grantham.

The maleness of the juvenile formation was another harbinger. It
was a man, her father, who prepared her for the man's world she
aspired to:

Wickstead:
She admired him enormously, that's the first thing. He was a
tall, dignified, white-haired man who was Mayor of
Grantham, and was chairman of our Governors. He was also
a Methodist local preacher and an Independent Councillor,
and very, very interested in politics – local and national. And
she always listened to him and admired him.

He set his daughters rigorous standards:

Foster:
The Roberts family were very strict Methodists and used to go
to Church twice or three times on Sunday. Mr Roberts himself
was a lay preacher in the Methodist Church, and used to go out
to preach in the villages around Grantham. Although he took a
daily paper he wouldn't, for example, take a Sunday paper,

until Margaret came home from university in the vacations, and insisted that they had a paper on Sunday, the *Observer* if I remember rightly.

Perhaps the fact that he did give way offers another clue to their relationship.

Wickstead:

He's sometimes been described as authoritarian. I would say that he probably was, but he was certainly not forbidding. He was a very kindly man, devoted to her and extremely proud of her.

Certainly her protestant work-ethic, so evident today, was learnt at his knee.

Wickstead:

I should imagine it came entirely from him, and so did her honesty and her integrity because Mr Roberts was a very courteous, straightforward, honest sort of man, much respected in Grantham, in fact perhaps at one time the most respected Grantham citizen, and I think he had an enormous influence on Margaret. He worked very, very hard, and indeed so did his wife, they both worked hard all the time. The story goes that they had no real family life. They were devoted to each other, but they never had the sort of meals when they all sat round the table together because father was so busy in the shop and in politics.

Alfred's politics may not have been identical to hers as they subsequently evolved; he seems to have been a believer in public spending, at least for the benefit of Grantham. However, there is no doubt her father was the decisive formative influence on her. Margaret Thatcher once described her mother as 'the Martha rather than the Mary',[1] and although she always worked in the shop – and therefore Margaret was brought up by a working mother – it is clear that Mrs Roberts kept very much in the background.

Wickstead:

Few people did know much about her mother. She was very much a homely person. I believe she sewed well, she was a good homemaker and perhaps, let's face it, she wasn't an academic in any way. Margaret admired academic ability as much as anything else, so I used to feel, just occasionally, that she rather despised her mother and adored her father.

---

[1] *Talking Politics*, BBC Radio 4, 31 August 1974.

Such academic purpose was almost bound to lead to Oxford, as it had done for many girls before her at the Kesteven and Grantham Girls' School. But there, too, the lineaments of the future politician began to be picked out: more clearly than those of the chemist she studied to be. The politician now trades, quite fairly, on being a scientist: but it is for politics more than chemistry that people remember her. Dorothy Hodgkin, later a Nobel prize-winner for Chemistry, was her tutor:

Hodgkin:

I came to rate her as good. One could always rely on her producing a sensible, well-read essay and yet there was something that some people had that she hadn't quite got.

Dame Janet Vaughan, another scientist, was head of her college, Somerville:

Vaughan:

I mean nobody thought anything of her. She was a perfectly good second-class chemist, a beta chemist.

But for her particular brand of political allegiance Margaret scored alpha as an original.

Vaughan:

She was extremely interesting to me because she was a Conservative. And the young at that time, especially in Somerville, were all pretty left wing. She wasn't an interesting person except as a Conservative. I used to entertain the young a great deal, and if I had amusing, interesting people staying with me, I would never have thought really of asking Margaret Roberts because she wasn't very interesting to talk to, except as a Conservative.

Another witness of her early years was Maurice Chandler. He served with her on the committee of the University Conservative Association, of which she became president in October 1946. He remembers her as an excellent party-giver:

Chandler:

When you were invited to a party she had arranged at Somerville, you could always be certain that the food and drink would last out – it wasn't always the case immediately after the war with some people – and you could also be certain that you would probably meet somebody you had never met before.

An ability that has, by all accounts, stayed with her all the way to No. 10. As have the other characteristics he noticed at the time.

Chandler:

Her attention to detail, her concern to ensure that a job was well done, her orderly and methodical approach to problems and indeed her organising ability.

Margaret Wickstead, who had left Grantham for Oxford a year ahead of Margaret Roberts, always thought her politically ambitious:

Wickstead:

She was single-minded from the beginning, and all the stories about her being rather a dull person as an undergraduate and at school may have been true. She was too concerned with her two things – her work and her politics. Politics was her thing and she just loved it, and she realised that chemistry probably wasn't the way into it. Soon after she'd taken her degree and got her second we were walking together down past Rhodes house and she said, 'You know, I've simply got to read law. It's no good, Margaret, chemistry is no good for politics, so I shall set about reading law.' And she did.

The first public record of her political earnestness dates from the 1945 General Election. Campaigning for the local Tory, she was described by the *Grantham Journal*[1] as 'a young woman of decided convictions'. Tantalisingly, the reporter doesn't say what the convictions were, but as Margaret Wickstead observes, the style was set:

Wickstead:

If she says, 'It's a fine day', she says it with conviction, the emphasis on the words every time. And the way in which she uses emphasis has been there a long time, ever since she started toying with the idea of being a politician.

There were, in fact, plenty of Conservatives at Oxford as the war was ending. Among these, the muted tone of upwardly mobile earnestness is better remembered in Margaret Roberts than any sign of today's flashing brilliance. Rachel Kinchin-Smith preceded her as a rare female president of the University Conservative Association:

Rachel Kinchin-Smith:

I remember her rather as a brown girl. She had an attractive brown head of hair, was quiet, nicely dressed and very pleasant to be with, but definitely other than the way one sees her today. It wasn't that she hid her light under a bushel. I don't think she had false modesties. I think that she just did a good job without any show among a group of young people who of course at that period of their lives enjoy show.

---

[1] 6 July 1945.

And how conscious was she of being a woman trying to penetrate a man's world? Perhaps not much. The main consideration, surely persisting to this day, was:

Rachel Kinchin-Smith:
. . . a deep, sincere and zealous wish to do well for her country. The roots of this wish, I would say, were more likely to be her Methodist background, which will have been fed by her discovery at school that she had abilities, and probably the most important way in which her femininity would come into it was that it gave her passion and endurance.

Rachel's husband, Michael, was another contemporary and was present at the creation of something with a very distinct modern resonance: just about the first known statement of Mrs Thatcher's political philosophy – the Oxford Tories' contribution to the ferment of argument within Conservatism after they'd lost the 1945 election. Mr Kinchin-Smith and Margaret Roberts were joint authors. It's a pretty po-faced document – but suggests among other things that today's attacks on consensus politics are no sudden invention.

'Conservative policy has come to mean, in the eyes of the public, little more than a series of administrative solutions to particular problems co-related in certain fields by a few unreasoning prejudices and the selfish interests of the monied classes. If this extremely damaging view is to be refuted it is essential that the relation between overall policy and the various solutions be shown and that the latter be demonstrably free from any suspicion of compromise between national and sectional interests.'

Zeal, industry, ambition, endurance, firmness of purpose: all these traits now seen in the Prime Minister can be traced back to her youth. So, according to Margaret Wickstead, can something else:

Wickstead:
I don't think she has much sense of humour. I don't think her father had, and I certainly don't think her mother had. They were all very very serious minded, they worked too hard. Life was a serious matter to be lived conscientiously and humour just didn't come into it very often. I have found personally that she hasn't a huge sense of humour. I wouldn't make a joke in her presence that might possibly reflect on her. I don't think I should be well received again.

She could neither enjoy a joke nor make one – a weakness for a politician. As Janet Vaughan recalls, Margaret's undergraduate solemnness was still dismally intact thirty years later:

Vaughan:
She came down to a Gaudy when she was Education Secretary, and she had to be asked to make a speech. A Gaudy is a gay time, as you know: good food and good drink and good speeches. Up got Margaret to make her speech. 'Hello, Somervillians and taxpayers', and she gave us a lecture on tax law. And this Somerville has never forgiven her for. But that is typical of her, you see, absolutely typical. I suppose now she'd have people who would protect her from doing that sort of thing.

Well, not entirely. This capacity not to understand when other people want to be a little light-hearted follows her still, right into the topmost councils of the world. Even her ardent admirer Ronald Reagan was a little miffed when he put her humour to the test:

Reagan:
I'm being a little reluctant here about telling something, and I hope it won't be tactless of me if I tell it. When we had the summit meeting here in our country, at Williamsburg,[1] which as you know has been restored to the original colony that it was, the first meeting was an evening meeting, dinner, to open the whole session, and it took place in what had been the British Colonial Governor's mansion. And I was going to suggest that had one of her predecessors been a little more clever, she might be hosting that gathering. And so we sat down; there was a moment of quiet before conversation broke out, and I said, 'Margaret, if one of your predecessors had been a little more clever . . .' She said, 'I know, I would have been hosting this gathering' . . . I never got to finish my line!

So there has been a kind of wholeness about Margaret Thatcher's formation: a very close identity between her public and her private character, her personal origins and her political performance. This is, in one sense, a discouraging starting point for our enquiry. Unlike many of her predecessors, she has few hidden depths and, one suspects, nothing much of a secret life. On the other hand, it begins to make her more completely explicable. Those like Sir Douglas Wass, who clashed intimately with her as

---

[1] 28–30 May, 1983.

Permanent Secretary to the Treasury from 1974–83 – a department on which she set her hostile sights from the beginning – are
as sure of the continuities as are her Grantham contemporaries:

Wass:
She is very much, I think, the product of her youth and her
upbringing. She was brought up as the daughter of a trader in
a difficult trading environment, saw all the problems of being a
businessman in the 1930s and she has a deep feeling for small
businessmen and people who are staking their livelihoods on
their activities, and she thinks that the state ought not to get in
the way of those sorts of people. It's a perfectly understandable point of view.

Nor has this identity between the public and the private life
grown less in her maturity. Alfred Roberts was replaced by Denis
Thatcher who married her in 1951 – replaced not exactly as
mentor, but certainly as friend and faithful prop. Much ridiculed
and even pitied, Denis Thatcher, according to Conservative MP
Sally Oppenheim, should not be underrated:

Oppenheim:
She is extremely lucky, and she would be the first to say so, in
that she has got a wonderful husband, who adores her and
who has been enormously supportive to her, who is an
immensely kind and thoughtful man and who she loves. So
she's got a very happy marriage and she's very lucky and I'm
sure she knows it and she wouldn't deny it. Denis has believed
in her in a very constructive way and thinks she's marvellous
and that everything she does is wonderful. He has a very kind
nature. He's a very much misrepresented man.

Sir Monty Finniston, who came to know the Prime Minister's
husband well when he was Chairman of the British Steel Corporation and Denis Thatcher was director of a subsidiary of Burmah
Oil and both companies had a fifty-per-cent share in a chemical
company, endorses that view:

Finniston:
I think her marriage has been a very stabilising factor for Mrs
Thatcher. The one friend she's got in the world, to whom she
can turn – and she must be under great stress most of the time –
is Denis Thatcher. He's a remarkable man, he really is, and I
think she'd be very grateful for that. And when all the rest of
the Party might not want her any more the one man that will
stay with her will be Denis Thatcher. He works well with her.
He understands her and he can cater to her – I use that in the

best possible way. I think he must be a remarkably calming influence when she is stressful and gets emotionally het up. I think he calms her down, she's very lucky.

Denis can also offer the kind of practical advice which few male prime ministers could expect from their spouses. Sir John Hoskyns, who worked as a senior adviser to Mrs Thatcher for four years, including two in No. 10, sees Denis's importance as stretching rather beyond emotional support:

Hoskyns:

She is married to somebody who has been in business all his life, does understand balance sheets, does understand how people tick, does understand the imperatives of business. I've very often heard her say on topics that have cropped up in nationalised industries and so on, 'Well, Denis looked at the balance sheet and said, "you know, there seems to be an awful lot of debt there which ought to be capitalised" or "why is the interest forgiven?" or whatever.' And because she's very quick on financial matters I'm sure she would instantly understand exactly what Denis was saying.

Denis has always been crucial to her. He's been beside her since her earliest days in politics. Apart from anything else, his money provided a security denied to most of her contemporaries. But the dependence was mutual and it did not become less so when she climbed the ladder – which she did when she became Secretary of State for Education in 1970. As Sir William Pile remembers it, not even the education budget was allowed to come between Denis and his breakfast – or between Thatcher the housewife and Thatcher the rising Cabinet minister:

Pile:

I was briefing her alone on a Wednesday before the Thursday's Cabinet when she suddenly stopped and said, 'What's the time?' I said, 'It's ten to five.' She said, 'Oh, I must go and get some bacon.' And I said, 'What do you mean?' She said, 'I must get Denis some bacon.' And I said, 'Well, the girls in the office outside can get it for you.' 'No,' she said, 'they won't know what kind of bacon he likes.' So she got up and she went down, she put her hat on, she put her coat on, I remember she put her gloves on because it was, after all, November, and she walked down to Clarges Street, across the road into Shepherd Market, bought apparently a pound of streaky bacon, came back into the office, took her gloves off, took her coat off, put the bacon down, sat down on the chair and said, 'Now, where were we?' So we resumed discussing the Chancellor's proposal that thirty million pounds should be cut off the education public expenditure bid.

Margaret Thatcher came to the DES via a junior job at the Ministry of Pensions and National Insurance which she held from 1961 to the 1964 General Election. Her boss there was John Boyd-Carpenter:

Boyd-Carpenter:
She was appointed a minister, albeit a junior minister, just over two years after getting elected to the House of Commons, which is pretty unusual except in wartime. Harold Macmillan, who after all ended up with six and a half years as Prime Minister, didn't get office at all for fourteen years after he came into the House of Commons.

He admits that at first he was cynical about why she had been singled out for office so soon:

Boyd-Carpenter:
I thought quite frankly, when Harold Macmillan appointed her as one of the two parliamentary secretaries at the Ministry of Pensions and National Insurance where I happened to be minister, that it was just a little bit of a gimmick on his part. Here was a good-looking young woman and he was obviously, I thought, trying to brighten up the image of his government. I couldn't have been more wrong because once she got there she very very quickly showed a grip on the highly technical matters of social security – and it's an extraordinarily technical, complex subject – and a capacity for hard work which she's shown ever since and which quite startled the civil servants and certainly startled me.

Macmillan's successor as leader of the Conservative party, Lord Home, never really had a great deal to do with her until six years later when they were Cabinet colleagues in the Heath government, she at Education, he at the Foreign Office:

Home:
I was struck then by her incisiveness in everything she said, and her grasp of her subject. She was never caught out, ever, by any question asked. So my recollection of her is quite clear. Curiously enough I came back one day and said to my wife, 'You know, she's got the brains of all of us put together, and so we'd better look out.'

But in many ways the best witness to her time at Education, and its role in her professional preparation, was not a political colleague but Pile, her Permanent Secretary. From the start there was an abrasive but lively relationship between them:

Pile:

Within the first ten minutes of her arrival she uncovered two things to us; one is, I think, what I would call an innate wariness of the civil service, quite possibly even a distrust, and secondly a page from an exercise book with eighteen things she wanted done that day. Now these were two actions quite unlike anything we'd come across from predecessors and later on I think we saw that this was only the beginnings of the revelation of a character that we'd have to get used to and that we hadn't run into before.

And instinctively she suspected that those eighteen policies which she wanted implementing immediately were things that the civil service would oppose.

Pile:

I think she probably did think we were going to make it difficult, but all I do know is the first point of the eighteen was that we should scrap the Labour government's circular urging all authorities to turn their secondary schools into comprehensive schools, and say quite plainly that you may if you wish retain grammar schools and even open new ones – and she had the draft of that circular on her desk that night. She said 'action this day' and she got it. We didn't stop to argue. This was a very clear political directive and we obeyed it, and so I don't think we did anything at the outset to make her feel that we were going to be obstructive. I think probably, though, as the weeks and months went by and we followed our old traditional course of speaking up for what either the Department had always done or what we thought the Department should do, as opposed to what ministers were going to tell us to do, she thought that some of us were being obstructive. I regarded it as a necessary professional job to be done up to the point when the minister said to you that we're going to do the opposite, in which case I think we touched our forelocks and said, 'Yes, Ma'am.'

This continuing, often acrimonious, dialogue with her officials forged an enduring attitude to the civil service as a whole.

Pile:

There were times, you know, when we did feel that her opposition was in fact to a degree due to a stubborn refusal to acknowledge some facts and arguments that we put forward.

It is a minister's right to be determined, but determination can turn into stubbornness. The other reason why I think she didn't really bother too much about one of the roles of the civil service, which is to offer advice, is that she didn't on the whole feel that she needed it. Her self-sufficiency was quite remarkable. Most senior civil servants feel that their principal objective or role is to offer ministers sound, balanced, neutral advice on the facts as they are known, given the objectives that ministers want to follow. I don't think she needed any of that. She never seemed to need any help. She just needed the facts. She evidently knew, without advice, what she thought about the facts. It appears that Mrs Thatcher, in the private world of the Education Department fifteen years ago, was behaving very much as now she is so famous for behaving in almost all circumstances.

Pile:

She is the only person I know who I don't think I've ever heard say 'I wonder whether'. Most of us, at moments of uncertainty or when faced with a lot of conflicting circumstances and confusion of objectives, will say, 'Well, what's it all about? What should we do? Any ideas? Should I do nothing? Should I do this? I wonder whether. . . ?' Now 'I wonder whether' was not a phrase that I ever heard on her tongue. So I think her self-sufficiency amounted to always having ready the answer in herself springing from her character. Equally, for that reason, she never seriously delegated anything. I asked her on several occasions, 'You know, this is quite a trivial matter, one of us can do that for you, if we get it wrong you can kick us in the bottom.' She said, 'No, I'll do it myself.' She worked to all hours of the day and night, she always emptied her box with blue pencils and marks on. Every single bit of paper was attended to the next day.

Nor was this the only forerunner of the prime ministerial style. The Education Department may have been a political backwater, but in it she gave expression to prejudices that would live on.

Pile:

She never really liked anything which was big, whether it was a local authority or a union or even a school. She didn't really care for comprehensive schools, but I think she disliked the size of them as much as their organisation as a comprehensive non-selective type of school. The reason I think she was wary of size in itself was that big bodies had a life of their own and she couldn't actually control them as easily as she could control small bodies, and obviously the civil service was a big body and had a life of its own and that's why I think she came in with a wariness about it.

The single most memorable thing Mrs Thatcher ever did at Education was to cut out free school milk for children over the age of six. This policy was not a Thatcher original. According to Sir William Pile she inherited it from a surprising source, Iain Macleod:

Pile:

Iain Macleod, as you know, was appointed Chancellor of the Exchequer at virtually the same time as she was appointed Secretary of State. He died soon after his appointment[1] but he left a sort of 'Last Will and Testament' on the back of an envelope which was immediately translated into gospel and everybody was implored to do what Iain would have done had he survived. On the list that was assigned to the Education front were three or four things, all of which had histories which are worth recalling. Iain Macleod had suggested that we abolish all free school milk. She did that very early on and of course, this led to the sobriquet of 'Thatcher the milk snatcher' and to a great deal of harassment and very unseemly bullying of her when she went to open schools. It did affect her but it never altered her decision that it was the right thing to do. The other things on Macleod's hit list were that charges should be levied on public libraries and museums. She left David Eccles[2] to decide whether to push through a charge on museums. He started to try to do so but in the end backed off. But she said from the outset that she would not countenance a charge on public libraries. I remember her saying that her father had regarded the public library as his university and that she wasn't going to prevent it being the same to anybody else. The other one on the Macleod list was to cut the throat of the Open University, and all I can say on that is after discussions of a variety of kinds she spared the Open University.

'Thatcher the milk snatcher' was the catch-phrase which finally dragged her out of obscurity into the front line of the cartoonists' victims. It was the first time she had really taken the heat.

---

[1] Iain Macleod was appointed Chancellor of the Exchequer on 20 June 1970. He died on 20 July 1970.

[2] Lord Eccles was Paymaster General, with responsibility for the Arts, 1970–3.

Pile:
I think it did hurt her. I think it was the first time she'd received abuse of this kind, I don't think she was prepared for it and it did get home. But she would never reveal anything in public; she was always a very good trouper, the show must go on, and she was always meticulous about turning up for meetings. If she said she'd be there at two minutes past six she'd be there at two minutes past six. She hid the hurt I think and no doubt like all such things it started callousing her, she built up a protective skin, she learnt that she had to, and I think she did so. There always has been a difference between her public impermeability and the fact that she's been hit internally.

The chief significance of this period, however, is actually that it was an aberration. Although there is an apparent continuity in Mrs Thatcher's personal and political record, her service under the Heath government was a rupture. No sign here of the future scourge of the public sector borrowing requirement, or, indeed, a minister interested in the economy at all. Jim Prior, later to spar constantly with her monetarist rigour, noticed nothing of that kind a decade ago:

Prior:
I can hardly ever remember her saying much which was not directly connected with education. For example, it would be quite wrong to think that she was against public expenditure or that she made great remarks about the increase in the money supply in the years '72 and '73. In fact she and Keith Joseph[1] were the big spenders in the Heath administration. It wasn't that they were saying the whole time 'we must cut back'. They were actually always asking for more.

Sir Douglas Wass, later to be the senior Treasury official in charge of carrying out her monetarist policies, recalls:

Wass:
My first encounter was in a Cabinet committee in 1971 or thereabouts when Mrs Thatcher was arguing for a larger slice of the public expenditure cake for Education and I at the time was supporting the Treasury minister.

John Biffen, who sat out the Heath government as an elegantly dissident right-wing backbencher, noticed nothing untoward in the Education minister's attitude to the government's general direction:

---

[1] Secretary of State for Social Services, 1970–4.

Biffen:

I don't think I had the impression that Margaret Thatcher was doing other than a highly competent job as Secretary of State for Education. I don't think that in that particular role she was given the opportunity to demonstrate these other economic and political attitudes, and it is my judgement that she did not engage in the sort of code messages which are very much in vogue nowadays. I think she just got on with the job that she'd been given and as such she was respected as a very competent and successful Secretary of State for Education. But I don't identify her with the great economic debate.

The great mystery, in fact, is exactly how and when the transformation took place. The first sighting of the Thatcher we now know, in rabid flight from her role as acquiescent accomplice in the Heathite corporate state, was recorded at a lunch at the then unfashionably right-wing Institute of Economic Affairs, where Ralph Harris, now Lord Harris of High Cross, was in charge:

Harris:

Whenever there was discussion of issues she would raise her voice and chastise her own colleagues. I can remember her falling on one rather stupid Conservative MP who was asking why we thought that people should value choice. She got up and spoke like a Finchley housewife about the choice of going shopping, and being able to go to one shop and then to another shop, and being able to make a choice, rather than being registered with the butcher as some of us remembered during the war, and having no choice. I remember how mercilessly she fell upon her own colleagues in that way.

It was certainly after the fall of the Heath government in February 1974 that any public recantation – with the slow emergence of the future mother of Thatcherism – began to display itself. Even then, she was far from being the leader of the band. Keith Joseph, an even bigger spender at the DHSS than she was at Education, was the first to see the light:

Joseph:

It's not a story of which I'm intensely proud because I should have reacted far sooner. Of course I should. I was too wrapped up in my job which isn't right for a minister. He should keep some of his energies for the big government policy issues. But I was wrapped up in my Health and Social Services job and I had cut myself off from old friends in the barbarous way that one is sometimes forced to do in government. When I went back to

pick up old friendships I found that Alan Walters[1] for example was very scornful, scarcely willing to talk to one because of what, from his understandable point of view, was a shameful failure to perceive error. And other friends took advantage of my new availability to explain the same thing to me. One particular friend, Alfred Sherman,[2] kept on emphasising to me that Keynes was dead and you can make more problems by trying to print your way out of difficulties than you solve. So it came about through a good bit of listening and a good bit of reading.
And Margaret Thatcher?

Joseph:

I'm sure that she was going through the same self-examination that many of us must have been going through. Why did it all go wrong? Each of us no doubt conducted the same sort of inquest in parallel, and I found that when I came to discuss this sort of thing, having rethought and reanalysed, Margaret Thatcher was totally in agreement.

This rethinking process didn't go unnoticed by their colleagues.

Prior:

As soon as the election of March 1974 was out of the way, there was no doubt about it that both Keith Joseph and Margaret began to work together and became, as it were, more and more isolated from the main trend of what the Conservative government had tried to do between '70 and '74. They came much more under the influence of Hayek,[3] and I always remember that when Keith Joseph made his famous Preston speech in the autumn – September – of 1974,[4] I was asked to see Margaret to see whether she could bring any influence to bear on Keith Joseph to stop him making it, and Margaret said, 'Oh, I don't know,' she said, 'I think Alfred' – and that I thought was significant, because it wasn't even Sherman, it was Alfred – 'I think Alfred has written it for Keith, and I think you'll find that Keith is now determined to make it, and I don't think I can influence him.'

Alfred Sherman, journalist, ex-Communist, tireless producer of

---

[1] Professor Alan Walters, Cassel professor of economics, LSE, 1968–76; professor of political economy, Johns Hopkins University, Maryland, since 1976.

[2] Sir Alfred Sherman, co-founder of the Centre for Policy Studies, 1974.

[3] The Austrian economist, Friedrich von Hayek.

[4] In Preston on 5 September 1974, Sir Keith Joseph, when he was opposition home affairs spokesman, rejected the bipartisan basis of postwar full employment policies, urging that in future priority should be given to the conquest of inflation by controlling the Budget deficit and the money supply.

rightist tracts, became an important influence in Margaret's life up to 1979 and, for a while, beyond. He denies that all she did was follow Keith Joseph:

Sherman:

Margaret Thatcher and Keith were close, but I never regarded her as being a disciple of his. She admired him, yes, but she wasn't a disciple. Her ideas came from elsewhere, above all from her instincts.

Equally, Lord Harris, who had challenged the economic consensus of the '60s and later for much longer than Sherman, doesn't think that her conversion came from reading:

Harris:

I've really puzzled over this because we saw a great deal of Keith Joseph and Keith Joseph was always to me a man who could as well have been in a university common room as in politics, and he – it goes right back to 1974 when he began to approach us about definite advice on reading – would go away with piles of books under his arm. And I'm certain that it's entirely through Keith Joseph that Mrs Thatcher was led to read and ponder our writings and our authors' publications. But she certainly isn't someone I can recall who ever came in to buy the latest Hobart Paper as Keith Joseph would do.

She was fired, in other words, by a combination of her own instincts and other people's ideas. But she had that indispensable political strength, which Joseph lacked: an eye for the main chance. When she filled the gap which Joseph left in the contest to unseat Ted Heath, it was against almost everyone's expectations. She was near the bottom – according to Jim Prior, who ran against her in the second ballot – of a pretty well-scraped barrel:

Prior:

I don't think anyone at that time really thought that Margaret was a serious contender. After all it was quite clear that Airey Neave and a number of others were determined to get rid of Ted, and they were going to try to find almost anyone to take on, and that's why they first of all went to Keith Joseph, and when he dropped out for some reason or other, then they actually approached Edward du Cann and he dropped out for some reason or other, so they were getting pretty desperate by then. There was literally no one else within the Cabinet or anywhere near the Cabinet who was prepared to stand against Ted Heath, unless Ted Heath said he was going to go.

Airey Neave had shared chambers with Margaret Thatcher in her barrister days, and they had been friends for years. Neave was to die tragically, murdered by Irish terrorists, at the beginning of the 1979 election. He had been, at least organisationally, the man who put her where she got. But he had early doubts. He thought she might suffer from being a woman. His widow, Lady Airey, explains that this made backing her a very big step indeed:

Airey:

My husband was not at all a lady's man. He had lived a great deal of his life amongst men, with his education, with Oxford, with the army, in Colditz, at the Bar. His life had been very much an active life, lived amongst men. So this was really almost a bigger decision for him than for some others. I think in the end he was influenced by the thing which had so largely governed the whole of his life, and that was the question of patriotism. I think he recognised that Margaret Thatcher thought in the same terms as he did, that the welfare of the country was the most important thing as far as they were both concerned. I think that had a very great effect on his choice and his decision to back her in her candidature.

Margaret Thatcher was at that time leading for the opposition on tax matters. When the Labour government's Finance Bill proposed a new Capital Transfer Tax, she seized her opportunity. Cecil Parkinson was the Conservative whip on the Bill:

Parkinson:

She made those very strong speeches which actually did quite a lot to establish her as a potential leader. Particularly in the second reading she made an outstanding speech. And that turned a lot of people's minds. It was very interesting, she'd totally dominated the House that day. She'd obviously mastered the subject and it was a big turning point for her.

Lady Airey was asked by her husband, who was tied up on the Committee corridor, to watch from the gallery:

Airey:

He asked me if I would go and listen to every word of the Finance Bill debate which was being largely conducted for the opposition by Margaret Thatcher, and I was immensely impressed. I went with an open mind entirely, and by the time I'd heard her final speech I felt no longer that I was listening to a man or a woman, but to somebody who had enormous grasp of the facts and had really got on top of the whole situation. He of course had been present for a fair amount of the debate but couldn't be there for the whole time, and I remember we had

long discussions into the night in which we both agreed that
her grasp of this very difficult subject of Capital Transfer Tax
was so immense that it didn't matter if she was a woman. If she
could deal with that she could deal with anything.

She certainly dealt with her once-superior colleagues. Being the
only one prepared to stand, she won. Her main opponent at the
finish was Willie Whitelaw, who had refused to stand against
Heath and was swept aside by the Thatcher bandwagon once he
got into the race on the second ballot.[1] Since then, Whitelaw has
become Mrs Thatcher's most valued lieutenant. Looking back,
was it a good thing she'd won?

Whitelaw:

It turned out to be so, most certainly, yes. Obviously I didn't
think so at the time. I wanted Ted Heath to remain. I don't
think I'd realised quite the extent of the feeling against him in
the parliamentary party, perhaps because I'd been away in
Northern Ireland for much of the previous time. But the fact
that he had lost the two elections, one in February '74, and
then again in October, underlined the fact that the parliamentary party really felt they'd had enough of him. I don't
think we'd all realised that, but it was very deep.

To represent this as a victory for ideas would be a mistake.
Thatcherism in February 1975 had not been born. Whitelaw
doesn't think her being a right-winger had much to do with it:

Whitelaw:

I don't think so. I think the truth is that she had the courage to
stand against Ted Heath, and it was a very remarkable decision
on her part. It is true that she had disagreed with many of the
things that he had done, although of course she was party to
them in the Cabinet, but she had disagreed basically, and she
wanted to see changes which I think many of his other colleagues didn't. I, for one, didn't.

David Howell was then an ally, and later entered her Cabinet as
Energy Secretary. The victory, he says, was an example of that
most common phenomenon in the annals of political change – a
simple response to failure and a desire to start again:

Howell:

In a sense, it was written in the stars. The thing was estab-

---

[1] In a first ballot on 4 February 1975 Mrs Thatcher won 130 votes, Edward Heath
119, and Hugh Fraser 16. In a second ballot on 11 February Mrs Thatcher won
146 votes; William Whitelaw 79; James Prior 19; Sir Geoffrey Howe 19; John
Peyton 11.

lished, once it was clear that Ted Heath was not going to survive. Willie Whitelaw standing was a noble gesture but it was pretty clear that he was not really going to win over this new force that had arisen, which represented a great many feelings hitherto suppressed and inarticulated in the modern Tory party. Lord Whitelaw doesn't dissent from this verdict:

Whitelaw:

I'm not sure that anyone really knew that the tide was actually there before she took it on and sought to ride on it. But once she had, she changed the argument of politics very much. She has changed the tone too in some ways. She has certainly brought out a feeling amongst a lot of people which must have been there below the surface, but wasn't appreciated before. It's a very remarkable achievement.

As Chris Patten, MP, then head of the Conservative Research Department, puts it:

Patten:

I think it was much more a peasants' uprisng than a religious war. It was seen much more as the overthrow of the tyrant king rather than as a great ideological shift. There were ideological arguments about what happened from 1970–4 but I think it was primarily a reaction of the parliamentary party against the fact they thought they had been taken for granted and that they'd lost too many elections.

That she was aware of this is verified by something she said to Sir William Pile in a moment of candour:

Pile:

I can remember asking her at one point what her ultimate ambition was, and she said, 'I would like to be Chancellor of the Exchequer but the Tory party will never allow a woman Chancellor of the Exchequer.' She clearly was wrong over that, but the fact that she thought it was an inhibiting factor is a revelation. Later on when she was leader of the opposition I wished her well for the next election, her first election of course,[1] and she said, 'Well, if I lose I will be out tomorrow,' and I said, 'Oh, come, come, the Tory party always lets you lose two elections before they fire you,' and she said, 'Not if you're a woman.' I think she was concerned that there was an inbuilt supposition in the Tory party that only a man would get to the top, which spurred her on. She was as surprised as any-

---

[1] The general election of 3 May 1979.

body when she won the contest for election to be party leader, far more so than winning the election. Then, once she got between the shafts, she thought, 'Well, if I'm the front runner I shall win the race,' and at the election she did.

Her win was not greeted with enthusiasm on all sides, and the lapse of time has not induced people like that most archetypal of anti-Thatcherites, Francis Pym – former chief whip, former Defence Minister, Leader of the House and Foreign Secretary, and a man who never ceases to ruminate in his tent – to revise the judgement he remembers making then:

Pym:

What worried me at the time was that for all her great qualities – which are many – she hadn't got the breadth of outlook that I felt a leader, a prime minister and leader of the Conservative party, needs to have. I didn't feel that she had the depth of thought that is really necessary. That is what particularly worried me, and I think actually, on the whole, it has been shown to be so, although as I say she has got some remarkable qualities which she has used to the benefit of Britain and the party.

An acid memory, not improved by what's happened to Mr Pym at Mrs Thatcher's hands in the meantime – she sacked him from the Cabinet after the 1983 election. As a contemporary record, perhaps we should look elsewhere. And where more revealing than in the diary of Barbara Castle – a woman with whose pugnacity and style Mrs Thatcher's has not a little in common? The entry in the Castle diary, written just before Margaret's accession to the leadership, captures that aspect of her which has most impressively survived the decade: her almost erotic excitement with the possession and the responsibilities of power:

Castle:

Wednesday 5 February 1975. The papers are full of Margaret Thatcher. She has lent herself with grace and charm to every piece of photographer's gimmickry, and don't we all when the prize is big enough? What interests me now is how blooming she looks. She has never been prettier. I am interested because I understand this phenomenon. She may have been up late on the Finance Bill committee, she's beset by enemies but she sails through it all looking her best. I understand why – she's in love – in love with power, success and with herself.[1]

---

[1] Barbara Castle, *The Castle Diaries 1974–6*, Weidenfeld and Nicolson, 1980 p. 303.

Over the Barricades

First Broadcast: 12 May 1985

Margaret Thatcher is a Conservative. But she would also like to be that entirely un-Conservative creature, a revolutionary. She's wanted to turn a whole lot of things upside down: not, of course, the democratic system, but the way government is done, what government is, what Conservatism still wants to conserve. A key to her performance has been her relations with other people in government: her colleagues, her party, her civil servants. How does she impinge on them? Well, first of all by being a woman. This was the first barricade she leapt over. Conservatives for the most part seem to regard the subject as the sort of thing gentlemen don't talk about, while on the left it raises all sorts of jangling contradictions which good feminists would prefer to avoid. Nevertheless, the gender question is a thread woven right through Mrs Thatcher's politics and behaviour.

People look at it very differently. Britain's first woman Prime Minister made an instant impact on foreigners. When Ronald Reagan first met her, she was leader of the opposition and he merely governor of California:

Reagan:
She was extremely well-informed, but she was firm, decisive, she had targets in mind of where we should be going. I was just greatly impressed. I know that there were some people who couldn't quite get used to the idea of a woman as Prime Minister, I doubt if there are many of those around any more. She's a great Prime Minister, not because she's a woman, but because of what she knows, what she does, and because of her insight into the right answers for the problems confronting us. I have never seen in any of our NATO meetings or summit meetings any lack of respect and recognition of her stature because she is a woman.

But even President Reagan wouldn't say it's possible to disguise the fact that she's a woman – which, if only in those numerous summit photo-calls, makes her stand out from the crowd. Some Americans, like Zbigniew Brzezinski, who was President Carter's national security adviser, briskly insist that this is little more than a sartorial accident:

Brzezinski:
In her presence you pretty quickly forget that she's a woman.
She doesn't strike me as being a very female type of woman.
Others, like Alexander Haig, US Secretary of State during the
Falklands War, have no doubt that she is, indeed, a female type of
woman:
Haig:
Every bit. From head to toe.
Sir Keith Joseph, who's known her a lot longer, is sure that this
matters:
Joseph:
She seems to have turned her very womanliness, and she is
very womanly, into an asset. She always looks very nice.
That's an asset.
The Thatcher appearance is certainly an important part of the
phenomenon. She took her place in a man's world soberly
dressed. As a child her school friends remember her as always
being neatly turned out. At Oxford the 'brown girl' image
remarked on by Rachel Kinchin-Smith in the previous chapter
was also noticed by the head of her college, Dame Janet Vaughan:
Vaughan:
She was a mousy person with mouse-coloured hair. She was
always rather neat. I mean her clothes were dark, neat, tailor-
made. The young at that time were pretty so that her neat
tailor-mades, always mouse-coloured, were fixed in my mind.
Later, in the early sixties after she'd got into Parliament, she
abruptly changed this image, becoming a blonde and adopting a
grander style. As her contemporary Margaret Wickstead put
it:
Wickstead:
I do know that she was the sort of person who always wore
court shoes and high heels and would even go round a country
farm in high heels if she possibly could.
For years the cartoonists rightly depicted her in large hats, an
image which sometimes, nevertheless, masked the formidable
woman underneath. Lady Airey remembers an occasion when
the fresh-minted Education Secretary came to carry out two
engagements in Airey Neave's constituency. One was to present
the prizes at Abingdon Grammar School and the other to visit the
Atomic Research Centre at Harwell.
Airey:
We arrived in good time to be there to meet her. She was look-

ing very attractive as of course she had to go on to this other engagement, and in those days you were expected to wear a sort of garden party dress and a hat if you were going to give away prizes as she was later in the day. And I remember so well the way the assembled company, all the young scientists who were there to meet her, looked with a certain cynicism on this young and attractive woman who had come to talk to them dressed in these very attractive garden party clothes. But then I noticed, as she started to talk to them, that their whole attitude completely changed and that they realised they were talking to someone who knew really all about their subject, and they were obviously very struck not only by her knowledge, but also by the homework which she must have done about the main projects at Harwell at that moment, and they were obviously very impressed by her.

Barbara Castle brilliantly observed the mixed effect Margaret Thatcher's appearance had on the men around her in a diary entry of 4 March 1975, three weeks after she became leader:

Castle:

Margaret's election has stirred up her own side wonderfully: all her backbenchers perform like knights jousting at a tourney for a lady's favours, showing off their paces by making an unholy row at every opportunity over everything the government does. Today they were baiting Harold over Reg Prentice's speech, and once again Harold was getting away with it, not by wit, but by sheer verbosity. Everybody kept glancing at Margaret to see when she would take him on. She sat with bowed head and detached primness while the row went on: hair immaculately groomed, smart dress crowned by a string of pearls. At last she rose to enormous cheers from her own side to deliver an adequate but hardly memorable intervention with studied charm. Roy J., sitting next to me, groaned and I said, 'She's not quite real, is she?' As he agreed, I added, 'If she would only occasionally come in with a smut on her nose, her hair dishevelled, looking as if she had been wrestling with her soul as I do.' He gave me his slow smile. 'I wouldn't say your hair is ever dishevelled. If that is to be the criterion, Shirley would win every time.' 'That's why everyone likes her,' I retorted. 'Men never feel at ease with a woman politician who looks as if her hair has just been permed.'[1]

---

[1] Barbara Castle, *The Castle Diaries 1974–6*, Weidenfeld and Nicolson, 1980 p. 330.

She came across striking evidence of the effort that went into this immaculate grooming, just over a year later.

Castle:

After I'd ceased to be a minister I used to do a lot of my work in the House in the little Lady Members' room at the back of the Speaker's chair, which had a few desks in it, and also a row of hooks. And I found to my astonishment that the row of pegs was always filled with Margaret Thatcher's clothes. There would be about half a dozen garments hanging up there and underneath them a tidy row of at least eight pairs of shoes. I can only assume that she slipped there from the opposition front bench, nipped into this little room and did her quick-change act between great parliamentary scenes.

Lady Airey confirms that organisation is the key to the Thatcher appearance; a characteristic she shared with Airey Neave himself:

Airey:

Airey always put his clothes out for the next day and laid them on the bed in the dressing room. That way you were completely prepared. And this is what I have very much noticed in the Prime Minister, that she is always ready and prefers to have everything totally in order the night before, rather than leave anything to chance on the day of the occasion. Ever since I've known her she has always been very organised and her clothes are always beautifully planned in advance, and actually it doesn't take any longer to do it, it just means that they're ready when you want to put them on.

But the importance of Thatcher the woman is by no means only trivial or cosmetic. Cecil Parkinson thinks it is central to her ability to link large issues of principle with their down-to-earth effects on everyday life:

Parkinson:

When, as Minister for Trade, I used to talk about the textile industry, I was working on this huge world-wide arrangement on textiles and multi-fibre agreements. Well, she could talk in terms of that but she could also relate it to buying material herself. I remember on one occasion when we were discussing it, she'd been out shopping the week before to buy some material and she'd noticed different foreign fabrics in the shops. Why were they coming here? And what was their attraction? So she would actually relate her shopping for materials to the multi-fibre agreement. Because she is a woman, she finds it easier to bridge that gap. And she does have this tendency to be able to relate the day-to-day rather more with the issue of principle or the complicated issue in front of her than perhaps some men would.

But it is in her relations with her peer group, every one of them a man, that gender can be of the most decisive importance. In the diplomatic world, for example, the combination of sex and aggression had a very unsettling effect when it first burst on Europe. The Belgian, Viscount Davignon, a vice-president of the European Commission from 1977 to 1984, recalls the early days of Mrs Thatcher's famous assaults on the Common Market budget, when the shuffling collection of her male antagonists was laid low by their natural good manners. It was a case of *toujours la politesse*.

Davignon:

What they did find harder is that they felt that it was more difficult to be rough with a woman than to be rough with another man. And so being challenged by a woman disconcerted them. If it had been a man they could have said, 'Shut-up.' They felt that they still had to be more polite to a woman. I think all that has taken care of itself now.

But if the foreigners have got used to it, nearer home gender is still a problem. Labour leader Neil Kinnock, facing Mrs Thatcher twice a week across the despatch box at Question Time, simply cannot bring himself to behave really badly:

Kinnock:

I think Mrs Thatcher is more difficult for me to oppose because she's a woman, because I suppose I respect women, and I've got, however much I try to shrug it off, an innate courtesy towards women that I simply don't have towards men.

Naturally it is on the men who work closest to her that the impact of her being a woman has been most powerful. Her deputy, Lord Whitelaw, is better placed than most to judge it:

Whitelaw:

She doesn't, I think, feel herself a woman amongst men. She did when she first came to be leader. She doesn't now at all. Nor do we any longer feel that we have to change our behaviour because she is a woman. Although I suppose, subconsciously, leaders in other countries – and perhaps even we ourselves – do somehow show more deference to a woman than we would to a man leader. Women get away with more with men than men do. We all know that, and I don't think she's in the least afraid to use the feminine touch to get her way if she wants to. She will use anything.

Jim Prior, a sparring partner for many years, and her Cabinet colleague as Employment Secretary and Northern Ireland Secretary, puts it more specifically:

Prior:

She had a degree of efficiency and no-nonsense about her, and up to a point, a ruthlessness in a strange sort of way, and I don't mean that in an unkind way because in many ways I found her to be very kind and very considerate, but she had a woman's attitude towards these things and a toughness towards these things, which I've never seen in a man.

All the same, it is not, according to the Labour veteran Denis Healey, entirely without precedent:

Healey:

The striking thing about her is that her imperiousness, which reminds me very much of Catherine the Great, or the Dragon Empress who presided over the terminal decline of the Manchu Dynasty in China, which is I suppose something for which you can find more women precedents than male precedents, is allied with a temperament which in many ways is very masculine. When she's tired she'll head straight for the sideboard and pour herself a stiff whisky and soda. She's happier arguing with men than with women, in fact I'm not aware of her ever arguing with women, or having very much to do with them. She's very much the sort of woman who does well in a man's world rather than a woman's world.

Some of her colleagues feel that even such a woman would benefit from some capacity, habitual in male politicians, to relax with cronies on equal terms. But Sir William Pile thinks that in her case this stems not from her gender but, like much else, from her character:

Pile:

I think she did lack male cronies. She did keep to herself and she fundamentally kept a distance from both men and women. She was in a curious way, not only very self-sufficient, but almost a loner because of that. In the end I don't think she needed anybody except herself which is a remarkable testimonial to anybody.

The world Denis Healey was talking about is, first of all, the world of the Conservative party. It is here perhaps that both these consequences of femaleness – the imperious aggression and the mealy-mouthed observance of social convention which prevents it being replied to in kind – have been seen at their most decisive. Julian Critchley, MP, a matchless chronicler of Conservative mores, suggests the trouble all began at public school:

Critchley:

At the beginning she was surrounded in the Cabinet by Tory gents and if Tory gents found a woman to be tiresome they swopped her for another. But it's Margaret that's been doing the swopping one way and another. I suspect that quite a number of people are frightened of her. And although the advice that you get if you go to see Margaret is 'stand up for yourself, shout back, and argue the toss and then she will respect you', the trouble is that that sort of advice to the English middle-class male of a certain age doesn't actually help us very much because we've always been brought up to believe that it's extremely rude to shout back at women. And we're reluctant to have rows. So she has been, to use a boxing metaphor, able to hold the centre of the ring, while the gents have scampered around the outside. There have been one or two exceptions – Willie Whitelaw has at times lost his temper with her – I wish I'd been a fly on the wall when it happened, and I think that she wouldn't have taken many liberties with Peter Carrington. But she is a bit of a bully.

Maybe Lord Whitelaw has a special dispensation. But on being asked whether his colleagues were frightened of their leader, he replied thoughtfully:

Whitelaw:

Don't know whether frightened of her is the right word. If you want to argue with her then you are advisably very careful to get your facts right and very careful to get your case right. And if being very careful means that you are rather nervous about the argument, then yes.

The response of her ministers to this environment has varied. How exactly they have related to her has, indeed, been one of the questions at the heart of her particular governing style. Lord Glenamara, who as Ted Short sat in a Labour Cabinet himself for four years, remembers a visit paid by Mrs Thatcher to Cable and Wireless, then a nationalised industry, which he chaired after leaving politics. His story is typical of dozens in circulation around Westminster and Whitehall.

Glenamara:

I thought it would be rather nice if she came along to see a really well-run publicly owned firm, a very successful one. She came to lunch with the directors, about a dozen well-informed, highly intelligent, articulate businessmen, and we started off a discussion, and throughout the whole lunch she wouldn't allow anybody to finish a sentence. She just chopped them off and sometimes got it wrong, sometimes anticipated the wrong question or wrong sentence. I've often wondered if she runs her Cabinet meetings like that.

David Howell speaks from experience. He discovered they weren't that different. In all Cabinets personal chemistry and political rivalry are ever-present elements. But the experience of combat, and its origins in the prime minister's personality, has seldom been so acutely felt as in the last six years. Howell, once one of her most favoured supporters, lasted only one term. For him, exile sounds as though it has some compensations:

Howell:

All I can speak for is my own relationship with Mrs Thatcher, which I don't think was a very close one and did involve a certain amount of loud argument and loud comment, some of which I confess I thought was unfair and misplaced.

Did he reckon that Mrs Thatcher enjoyed argument? After all, she'd said before getting to No. 10 that she wouldn't have time for it.

Howell:

Do you know, I don't really know? I used to think perhaps that that was the right way. If argument was the currency, then argument there should be, but of course, some arguments just left such acrimony and ill-feeling that I can't believe they really could have been enjoyable. I don't know, I find it very difficult. My own view about a great many public policy decisions is that clashes of interest do arise, but on the whole one wants to be discursive not argumentative unless forced to be. I think the general atmosphere in the government of which I was a member was that everything should start as an argument, continue as an argument and end as an argument.

Hardier spirits than David Howell look back on the era of argument more fondly, even when, like Jim Prior – never the true Thatcherite Howell once was – they were almost always on the losing end of it.

Prior:

The Cabinet in the first eighteen months to two years was certainly the best Cabinet that I've been in from the point of view of argument and discussion. There was a real debate on a whole range of matters, the issues were very well thrashed out with some very heated discussions, and I think that was good, although nearly always the side that I was on finally lost the vote, insofar as there are votes, they are not properly taken and counted.

Argument was the norm, certainly up to 1981 when the Prime Minister still had to contend with heavyweight opposition in her own Cabinet, and when Prior had a number of like-minded colleagues.

Prior:

It was a much more evenly balanced Cabinet in those days and the argument really was put very fairly and squarely, and to give Mrs Thatcher her due, she allowed the argument to take place in Cabinet. It was never quite such a balanced argument as the characters of personalities in Cabinet might suggest, because some people contracted out of the argument. But there were a number, I suppose, Norman St John Stevas, Ian Gilmour, and myself, to mention three, but there were others as well, who really did play quite a big part in it.

Those three have since left the Cabinet, and it now bears a more direct imprint of Mrs Thatcher's own priorities. But arguments are still a feature, essentially because the Prime Minister has a natural tendency to argue everyone into the ground. They are, are they not, simply a way of winning? Lord Whitelaw:

Whitelaw:

Oh yes. Certainly. Nobody could deny that. Everybody likes to win arguments. She likes to win them rather more than many others.

And doesn't change her mind?

Whitelaw:

Interestingly, she is prepared to change her mind far more than most people ever realise. Provided you argue with her on a case from the start she can be very easily convinced, I think perhaps more in big things than in small things. But on big issues most certainly, yes.

This is not how the process has struck everyone. Francis Pym recalls an atmosphere in which argument changed little or nothing:

Pym:

I think it's true that she has wanted to impose on the country her own view of things, particularly in the economic field, and although of course there is discussion and on many matters voices are heard and listened to, I would think that in her case it makes much less difference to the outcome than in the case of any previous prime minister. She was quite clear as to what she wanted and didn't take much to different views, and it was very rare that a Cabinet actually overturned what she wanted. I am sure it has happened on a number of issues, in fact I can recall some, but they are comparatively minor. But the style of it and her attitude to the House of Commons and so forth is very much one of 'this is what I want to do, this is what the country needs, and that's it' and any argument to the contrary tends to get brushed aside.

It does all depend where you make the argument from. If you are not an occupant of the *salon des refusés*, but a former economic adviser like Sir Alan Walters, for whom Thatcherism came only just in time to save the nation, the environment at No. 10 is alive with openness and flexible rigour – although Walters has the grace to concede that he had an easy ride:

Walters:

To say that she is not open to argument and not open to logic is absurd. She's more open to argument and logic, I think I'd say unequivocally, than the majority of politicians I know. You may say that this is just because she is susceptible to my arguments – perhaps so. But she followed my cases and she followed them I thought very well, far better perhaps than any other politician I've ever known, with the possible exception of Enoch Powell of course.

There is a pithier way to describe this temple of platonic dialogue. It comes from her former parliamentary private secretary, Ian Gow. There is a reason, says Mr Gow, why self-doubt has seldom been high among Mrs Thatcher's characteristics:

Gow:

The truth of the matter is that in my experience she was almost always right and therefore there wasn't a great necessity for her to admit she was wrong.

A fortunate circumstance, given the personal domination, argument or no, which she has established over the Cabinet. David Howell wonders how much of this is image and how much reality, but has no doubt that she revels in being number one:

Howell:

I think she does stand out, does she not, whether people are for her or against her, as an individual and as a dominant character in all discussion of British politics, in a most remarkable way? I don't know whether the Prime Minister ever planned this, but there emerged in the press the view that she was alone in the Cabinet surrounded by all these old women. I think there was a phrase the Prime Minister used which may have encouraged that impression. Didn't she say something to the effect that she was 'the opposition in her own Cabinet'? That must have greatly encouraged this feeling around that she was alone amidst a sea of fumblers.

The accusation, which this begins to amount to, that under Mrs Thatcher the British parliamentary system is being superseded by something closer to a presidency, has often been heard. It's the portentous way of saying that Mrs Thatcher is a one-woman band. Older hands from Whitehall are divided about this. Lord Bancroft, head of the civil service until he took an abrupt early retirement in 1981, thinks there has been a change:

Bancroft:

All leaders of all parties in my experience have carried, and have needed to carry, authority and respect – what is called in the jargon the grovel count – and I think that in this particular administration as I experienced it, it was a bit higher than it had been in some others. It's also the case that more and more of the levers of effective power have been hauled into the centre of the executive, particularly of No. 10 and the Cabinet Office.

Reg Prentice, from the unusual vantage point of having served in both Labour and Tory administrations,[1] contrasts Mrs Thatcher's style with that of Jim Callaghan who, he says, chaired the Cabinet and Cabinet committees not by domination but by drawing out the sense of the meeting:

Prentice:

I think he was better there than either Wilson who preceded him or Mrs Thatcher who followed him. I think her tendency is to state her own view, then perhaps someone else gets a word in, then she comes back and criticises them, and it goes on a bit like that instead of a drawing together a consensus of the meeting. And too many sessions are like that. In other words the style is too presidential. Now I think the British constitution has been changing anyway over the time I've been in

---

[1] Secretary of State for Education 1974–5; Minister for Overseas Development 1975–6; Minister of State (DHSS) 1979–81.

politics. The old idea that the prime minister was the first among equals has given way, step by step, towards a more presidential situation. I'm not happy about that and I would criticise a lot of prime ministers for their part in that process. But I think it has accelerated in Margaret Thatcher's time.

As Minister of State in the DHSS, he found the grovel count wasn't confined to officials:

Prentice:

I think there was an inclination in my department and in other departments to say, 'Well, the prime minister's view is so and so, and therefore we ought not to go against it.' I remember saying to some of my colleagues once that she's not a president, she's a prime minister, and that it's the Cabinet that makes the decisions and she doesn't. I forget what the occasion was, but I was in that mood from time to time. I'm an admirer of Margaret and was glad that she had strong views but I felt it was our job collectively as ministers to insist that other points of view were discussed and would prevail if enough of us felt that way, because our government should be a collective government and not too much a personalised government.

Chris Patten, currently Minister of State at the Department of Education, also sees dangers in over-personalised government:

Patten:

Clearly parts of the down-side of a Shavian[1] approach to politics of a very successful, vital, dominating leader is that so much of the energy and vitality, both political and intellectual, of a government depends on one person. And I think that is, inevitably perhaps, very largely the case today. I am sure that one of the things that the prime minister will be having to think about in the next few years and wanting to think about is how occasionally to change gear and how occasionally to throw the spears to other people to carry.

But Sir Douglas Wass, who was head of the Treasury until 1983, sees nothing particularly new in the presidential style:

Wass:

I doubt whether it's a trend. I think the extent to which prime ministers behave like presidents and the extent to which they

---

[1] George Bernard Shaw, 1856–1950, playwright and Socialist author, took the view that history was largely made by the individual actions of great men and women. See also page 139.

behave like chairmen of committees, varies almost randomly with the occupant of No. 10. A good example I think is Harold Wilson, who was quite presidential in his first administration and was very much the chairman in his second. You can pick on Winston Churchill, for instance, as an example of a very presidential form of government, certainly in those areas of government he was interested in, both during the war and immediately afterwards, and then you had Mr Attlee who was a very chairman-like prime minister. It's gone up and down over the course of history and I think it's quite possible we could revert to a chairman-type prime minister again.

Indeed, to her keenest supporters – such co-revolutionaries as her one-time *éminence grise* Sir Alfred Sherman – all she's doing is to compensate for the insidious weakness of most prime ministers vis à vis their colleagues.

Sherman:
The prime minister is, by the nature of things, weaker than the prime minister was fifty years ago when state expenditure was much lower and there were fewer ministers and fewer spending ministers. The only real spending ministers then were the armed services, so that ministers were less influenced by their civil service and were less likely to gang up against the prime minister over economic issues. What she has tried to do by personal ascendancy is to offset the tendency towards the weakening of the prime minister.

To this end, she has, as well as dominating the argument, dominated the lives of her ministers, and of the governmental machine set up to serve them and her: the civil service. This, surely, will be one of her most enduring and in some ways admirable marks. She has taken seriously the constitutional principle that the bureaucratic machine must be the servant of elected politicians. Another way of putting that would be to say that she has used extraordinary methods to insert herself into as many crannies of Whitehall as her questioning pen can reach. But to what was all this fabled critical activity mostly directed? Jim Prior remembers painfully:

Prior:
. . . towards the jargon and the obfuscation which the civil service and perhaps a minister, an unwary minister, would try to bring into the thing. She'd just write on the side, 'That is gobbledygook.' I tell you one thing that I found very interesting – the sort of letters that were sent round by her private

secretaries to ministers' principal private secretaries were a good deal sharper and more pointed than in the Heath period. I was quite amazed at the rudeness of the letters that came round as compared to the earlier time. They weren't couched in that sort of diplomatic language which they used to be couched in. This I think was Margaret saying, 'Be blunt. Don't beat about the bush.'

The most visible victims of this injunction have not in fact been ministers like Prior but civil servants. The upper bureaucracy, fount of consensus wisdom, has been toppled from its pedestal: sometimes, indeed, identified as the enemy not the ally of Thatcherite government. According to Sir William Pile, this tendency was always there. Mrs Thatcher didn't see the civil service as a machine, but as a collection of individuals, most of them less than adequate:

Pile:

She made up her mind about people very quickly and didn't change it. She once said, 'I make up my mind about people in the first ten seconds and I very rarely change it.' I think my experience bears out that that was true. When she made up her mind you were consigned either to a very short list of saints or a very long list of sinners and that was the difficulty, you couldn't work your passage from one side of the list to the other except in very exceptional circumstances.

Of all British institutions, not even the trade unions have suffered more than Whitehall from her capacity for unflinching scorn. Which is a little unfair, according to Lord Bancroft, since Whitehall turns out to have positively applauded the 1979 election result.

Bancroft:

When Whitehall is contemplating an election campaign being fought, its mood – I speak from my own personal experience anyway – is one of grim relish about the outcome. The relish is all the greater if the outgoing administration has been suffering from end-of-term palsy, the debility of no working majority. So in 1979 there was a positive welcome, on no party political grounds whatever, for a new administration with a mandate, with firm policies and with a defined profile to it.

But the honeymoon didn't last and even through the agonised circumlocutions of the mandarin the hideous truth emerges.

Bancroft:

I think there was a greater attenuation of the intimacy of

relationships between senior advisers and ministers than there normally is. And so the personal relationships between senior advisers and some ministers were rather cooler, rather more formal than they might otherwise have been.

Sir Frank Cooper, then Permanent Secretary at the Ministry of Defence, says Whitehall was slow to realise what was happening:

Cooper:

I think the idea that things were going to be different, that people were expected to behave differently, took quite a long time to percolate. What started it off was the series of visits she paid a few months after she took office in 1979, and the word about those visits went around Whitehall quite quickly. She went to quite a number of departments. They were inquisitions, but I think the cardinal point was that she demonstrated beyond peradventure that she was in charge.

The DHSS was one of the earliest departments to be visited. There, the Permanent Secretary was Sir Patrick Nairne.

Nairne:

She arrived towards the end of the morning. She walked round the department with great vigour and charm, meeting as many of the staff as she could. She lunched in the Secretary of State's room with ministers and the permanent secretary and the two second permanent secretaries. And she then had a discussion of the main policy issues. She very much led from the front throughout the occasion. We felt ourselves, perhaps wrongly, that our main role was to brief her about some of the problems in the department. She certainly raised plenty of questions with us, but we were less successful than we should have been in getting across some of the problems and pressures we saw in dealing with the policy on our front.

According to Sir Frank Cooper, all her relations with civil servants have to compete with an unbending prejudice:

Cooper:

I think she instinctively dislikes anybody who is not helping in the wealth creation process. I'm not sure she dislikes civil servants in their own right. I don't believe she does. But I don't think that she regards them as a group of people who are contributing to the wealth of the nation.

It took some time for the implications of this to dawn on Whitehall: an example perhaps of the very thing Mrs Thatcher was determined to break down – the invincible complacency of the place.

Cooper:

If you go back to my early days in the civil service after the war, what was happening then was that the real size of the civil service grew very fast in the post-war world when we had all the nationalisation and there was a belief amongst politicians and indeed amongst civil servants that they could do anything. We've come, I think, during her time as prime minister, to the opposite end of the pole when the civil service worries greatly whether there's anything it can do really well. So you've gone over a period of, I suppose, thirty-five, forty years, from one end of the spectrum to the other.

Sir Frank feels that the prime minister's sensitivity to this has not been as great as it might have been:

Cooper:

I've got a great deal of sympathy with the need to modernise the civil service, to reduce the amount of government we have, and to reduce the numbers in the bureaucracy. Where I am a critic is that, even if you accept these legitimate goals, it's not necessarily the best way of bringing those aims about, simply to knock everybody all the time. Frankly, one would like to have seen more positive leadership and a more generous meed of praise from time to time where work is well done by people who still work extraordinarily hard, particularly at the top of the service. So she wouldn't score the highest possible marks by any manner of means.

Perhaps civil servants are as much to blame as Mrs Thatcher for the sour relations which, with some exceptions, continue to characterise the government machine. Certainly Sir Patrick Nairne, who now runs an Oxford college, doesn't think it's entirely her fault:

Nairne:

I think, to be frank, that she's often not a very good listener. So I think the civil service was sometimes overkeen when they met her and discussed problems with her to seize the opportunity of getting across the difficulties that they felt might be obstacles to the achievement of policy objectives. Perhaps the civil service from this point of view was a bit over-defensive, but because this was the way things worked, it increased her feelings that the civil service were not the good partners that she wanted. I think she has always tended to be critical of those she felt were over-defensive or over-negative in their approach.

In other words, for all their griping, they'd have been better off standing up for their versions of the wisdom more bravely – or, possibly, being more like politicians, rather than mimicking the bloodless image which the typical civil servant carries around with him. One official who made his reputation with Mrs Thatcher by standing up to her was Sir Anthony Parsons, Ambassador to the UN during the Falklands crisis, who later became her foreign policy adviser at No. 10. He thinks she likes people who fight their corner:

Parsons:
Certainly in my own experience, yes. I've disagreed with her, stood up to her, on many many occasions over many many different subjects. I've never found her either pompous or hierarchic or resentful about it. Obviously she may violently disagree, but in my experience she has always welcomed really strong expression of view, even if it's totally contrary to her own.

In the last chapter Sir William Pile identified part of Mrs Thatcher's problem with civil servants as her own self-sufficiency, which makes their traditional advisory role superfluous. Denis Healey makes that point more sharply:

Healey:
I think that she has a very good brain – there's not the slightest question about that – when she wants to use it. The trouble is she also has an invincible complacency about her ignorance. She will not listen unless she's compelled to and there are only a few people she will listen to. She will listen to a civil servant who's not competing with her, particularly if she likes his personality. She rather likes sassy people like Peter Middleton[1] and they've done well under her, and I think she will listen if she feels somebody knows something about a problem which she knows nothing about. But she will never recognise in public that she's ignorant and this is a damaging thing in a politican.

Certainly one thing which no one would dispute about Margaret Thatcher is that she is completely a politician: a fighter for causes, a constant manoeuvrer for advantage, a blood-and-guts performer whenever she's under attack and often when she's not. Through radio, her House of Commons performances have made

---

[1] Peter Middleton succeeded Sir Douglas Wass as Permanent Secretary to the Treasury in March 1983.

her style better known than that of any prime minister in history, save possibly Churchill. What she lacks in subtlety she makes up for in volume – and it makes the Liberal leader David Steel cringe:

Steel:

I don't personally like her House of Commons style. I don't think that the 'fishwife' approach to the House of Commons is at all effective or impressive, but some people find it impressive.

Among them the Leader of the House, John Biffen, a man of almost infinite subtlety himself, but capable of seeing virtue in a different style:

Biffen:

I think that a good left hook comes naturally to the prime minister, and she exhibits those pugnacious skills to the delight of her parliamentary supporters. I think it's obviously a very very different style from, say, Harold Macmillan who had a most relaxed attitude, rather good natured and patronising towards the opposition, a totally different style. I think that the way she conducts prime minister's Question Time is to her great advantage with the parliamentary party.

From time to time she has varied this style. In the spring of 1985, her public relations advisers – and probably she herself – became worried by her reputation for stridency. She vowed to stop shouting. But it didn't last long. Labour's deputy leader Roy Hattersley, indeed, thinks such a break with her natural character would deprive her of her greatest advantage:

Hattersley:

She believes in attack and that is a great virtue. When Mrs Thatcher is cornered Mrs Thatcher does not defend herself, Mrs Thatcher attacks the people who have cornered her and I suppose that's as near as she gets to having an admirable quality. Her second House of Commons virtue or advantage is the sheer intellectual insensitivity with which she performs. Let me give you an example of what I mean – most people, when they are answering questions in the House of Commons or making a speech outside, actually do not want to give answers or make points which their more intelligent friends might regard as being foolish or wrong. Such considerations never influence Mrs Thatcher. She will make the best point to score the best advantage with the audience which concerns her at the time. So if somebody asks her a question which she finds it difficult to answer, the fact that her adversaries are hooting at her because she is not even attempting to answer it, will not deflect her at all. She will just say what is pragmatically best for her cause and her case. Now, as I say, I don't believe that would qualify her for high intellectual distinction, but it does show a political determination, a narrowness and at the same time a specific determination to win through politically, which is an enormous advantage in the House of Commons. An even closer student than Roy Hattersley is his leader, Neil Kinnock. He is less impressed. To him, she has simply mastered a game.

Kinnock:

Mrs Thatcher is copiously prepared and she gets the last word, but she's not very good on her feet. She's got one trick which consists of repeating the line the questioner has asked, and that's really the only oratorical skill she displays. Prime Minister's Questions, in any event, are somewhat overrated as gladiatorial contests, and people mistake them for politics.

At the heart of this technique, he suspects, is that old problem which Ian Gow earlier defined as her greatest virtue: the fact that she is sure she is almost never wrong.

Kinnock:

I think Mrs Thatcher would be much more comfortable as a governor of a country without an opposition. Characteristically, the idea that you test and examine and press, or that you quote her words back at her, are discomforting for Mrs Thatcher. And discomforting because she gives the impression, I might be inaccurate in this, that you actually don't have a right to ask these questions, which I think is evidence of lack of self-confidence and a certain frenzied attitude towards affairs rather than of any lack of competence.

This dislike of questioning is expressed in one other way. It is, in a sense, the organising principle behind the very selection of the people she will allow close to her. They may argue, but they must fundamentally agree. 'Is he,' she asks of any potential recruit, 'one of us?' Peter Shore is horrified:

Shore:

I'm sure that loyalty matters enormously to her. I think 'Is he one of us?' is one of the most remarkable phrases that has ever come out of a prime minister in Britain. In a sense it's almost as though she thought of herself as being one of a small band of pioneers and conspirators that found themselves in a kind of minority, an exposed position in Whitehall and Westminster, and that they had to stick together as a club in order to get the great machinery of state to be responsive to their new and radical approach.

The point about this club is not just that it keeps socialists and civil servants out, but Tories as well. The wrong sort of Conservative is the first to be blackballed. And that includes not just dissident Conservative backbenchers like Julian Critchley but, as he recalls, Cabinet members as well:

Critchley:

She used always to say of Michael Heseltine when his name was mentioned, 'Michael,' she used to say, 'he is not one of us.' And that phrase 'he is not one of us' ought to be the title of any book about what has happened to the Conservative party between 1979 and 1985. It tells you all you want to know. She felt under siege. She felt that by and large the bulk of the more intelligent or leading Tories were hostile to what she was trying to achieve, therefore she became defensive and was forced back into the position when she relied, and does rely increasingly, upon relatively small groups of people who think the same way.

What 'thinking the same way' adds up to is a puzzling business: everyone knows, but few can describe it. Cecil Parkinson, the former Party Chairman, a devoted Thatcherite and definitely 'one of us', claims the credit for originating the phrase:

Parkinson:

I think it means above all a real commitment to the Government's central economic strategy, the fight against inflation, the need to control public expenditure, all those things. It means solid opposition to trying to spend our way out of trouble, the dash for growth syndrome. There are, within that definition, quite a lot of variables on other matters. For instance on capital punishment: quite a number of the people who would be regarded as amongst the prime minister's staunchest supporters don't share her views on issues like that. So it doesn't mean an identity of view on everything, it means a commitment to the basic economic strategy and the sort of society that the prime minister and other Conservatives envisage.

Not all other Conservatives, but too many for Francis Pym, who raised the standard for the rest when he founded a pressure group on the Tory left, Conservative Centre Forward, in May 1985:

Pym:

She's certainly got the Tory party very much into her way of thinking and certainly has the loyalty of all the activists and the whole party in the constituencies. That is actually deserved because she's been extremely courageous and very strong and the first woman prime minister. In 1979 the country felt what a mess we were in and here was she leading it all, so she certainly has done that. But I also feel that it has been done in a way that is intolerant of other views and of criticism or other suggestions. She's used part of her personality to impose this particular style and this particular policy on the country and my concern has been that all the other views which exist within the Conservative party tend to be pushed to one side or ignored or turned down. It's that style that concerns me because over a very long period of time, a century and a half, the Conservative party has been more in government than out. It has been a remarkable political party for the country and it's done that by having very broad shoulders, by being able within itself to contain a whole range of views well to the right of Mrs Thatcher, well to the left of anybody else you like to suggest. And it's by accommodating all these views, indeed it is by sorting out these views within ourselves, that we've been able to serve for the nation as a whole over a long period of time.

From across the floor of the House, Denis Healey has observed this change reflected in the Conservative Members of Parliament:

Healey:

I think, basically speaking, she's hijacked the Tory party from the landowners and given it to the estate agents. Some of the things she's done were overdue in the Tory party. There's no question that the forelock-tugging Conservative voter is now replaced by an aggressive person who wants to make a fast buck, and she represents that part of the country. The trouble is the bucks aren't being made very fast.

Behind this decidedly snobbish formulation Mr Healey is talking about a set of policies: the policies of Thatcherism, to which end the assaults on the government machine are merely a means. Former Party Chairman John Gummer denies there's any truth in the crack about landowners and estate agents:

Gummer:

Well, some people invent a line like that and then justify it. It is the kind of line which one would like to have said oneself. It isn't actually true but it's too good to miss. I don't think that's what she's done at all. What I think she has done is to make the Tory party a party in which philosophy and some real intellectual input is important again. She has helped to win the intellectual argument all over the country in a way which perhaps previous prime ministers haven't. What she's done is actually to become the spearhead of the philosophical argument and now I find that one very often argues from the philosophic rather than from the practical base, which is a change that has brought the Tory party back to a Disraelian view. That's why she's much closer to Disraeli than she is ever thought to be.

There is intense competition for the Disraelian inheritance. Most of the Tory wets would certainly not concede it to Mrs Thatcher without a fight. One thing she does have in common with Disraeli, however, is the attention she pays to party management, especially in the House of Commons. She goes to great trouble to keep in touch with her backbenchers, cajoling and educating all the time. She doesn't wish to fall into the negligent ways of Ted Heath, who, when he was prime minister, was much disliked for failing to consult them – or even, in some cases, know their names. No such hauteur for Margaret. The man whose main job it is to keep her party relationships in good working order is her parliamentary private secretary. Ian Gow, also 'one of us', who did the job with notorious dedication for four years,[1] conjures up a picture of touching late-night intimacy with the proles:

Gow:

Of course she loves the House of Commons. She likes to get to know her backbenchers and most certainly she did get to know them. And she used to love to go down to the cafeteria, which is the least grand of all the places where one can eat in the House of Commons, where the more lowly backbenchers who didn't like to go and eat in the Members' Dining Room were. It's a very relaxed and informal atmosphere. The prime minister used to stand in a queue with a tray and wait for her buck rabbit and sometimes have a grapefruit before. And we always used to gather up Conservative MPs who were down there or go and sit at their table. And if you're just sitting down in a cafeteria with your tray in front of you and happy to help yourself to knives and forks, it's a very informal atmosphere and rather a good atmosphere in which to have a chat.

It must be reported, regrettably, that there are mixed feelings

---

[1] 1979–1983.

about this ritual. For one thing it doesn't always take place down in the cafeteria but sometimes up in the dining room. For another, according to Julian Critchley, its political effects are not unfailingly positive. It's evidently a greater pleasure to dispense than to receive the Thatcher mode of table talk:

Critchley:
I have on occasion sat at a table which she has joined for lunch, a table shall we say of five rather cheerful Members of Parliament drinking rather bad claret and gossiping. Suddenly you look up and the first thing you see is the sight of the prime minister's parliamentary private secretary, in those days it was Ian Gow with the sunlight glinting in a sinister fashion from his spectacles, and you knew that this was the harbinger of trouble. And then in she would come, she would sit down and everybody would stop talking and then she'd look at you and she'd say, 'Julian, what are your views on the money supply?' And all your gastric juices would begin to churn in the most frightful way, and you would stumble out some fatuous remark which she would then dismiss, and then she would turn to your neighbour and say, 'And what are your views on X, Y and Z?' Before the poor chap had a chance to answer, she would have interrupted him and immediately set off on some other discursive subject. So the whole business of having either lunch or dinner with Mrs Thatcher is, I think, to be avoided. Everybody's attempting to outdo each other, and to shine in a beastly way. I would avoid it like the plague if I were you.

Poor old Critchley. An old-fashioned sort of Tory. Weary, wet and witty, he's everything Mrs Thatcher has least time for. Next we turn to look at some of the things which, having stormed the barricades, she's done: to the economy, to society, to Britain's standing in the world. Done essentially on behalf of a new kind of Conservative party where the Critchleys have only a marginal place, for they have been among the conspicuous victims of a revolution which, its leader insists, is by no means over.

Good Housekeeping

First Broadcast: 19 May 1985

Thatcherism consists of a set of ideas about how to run the economy. Because this has become the recognised label for a political philosophy, and because it is a self-conscious break with the pragmatism of the past, its creator and embodiment has acquired a reputation for being, by comparison with her predecessors, uniquely interested in ideas. Margaret Thatcher is even called, by some people, an intellectual. Certainly, anyone looking for her personal contribution to economic policy must begin by asking where she got it from.

One reason why this reputation as a philosopher has clung to her goes back to the undisputed fact that she has consorted with gurus. But does this make her a creative thinker, in the way the 'ism' of Thatcherism would imply? Her political opponents look upon her intellectualism with different degrees of seriousness. Peter Shore, himself an economist, is not dismissive:

Shore:

In a curious way she is much more interested than her Chancellors of the Exchequer have been in simple economic theory. She really will enthusiastically tell you about the books she's read and the great panjandrums of the intellectual right, the economic right – Friedman,[1] Hayek.[2] These are people to whom she pays earnest and indeed almost passionate respect in conversation. She has deeply imbibed from them and she does believe that she is carrying out a policy according to the best wisdom of what she thinks are men of the utmost intellectual distinction.

But Roy Hattersley, Shore's successor as Shadow Chancellor, is more scornful than his colleague:

Hattersley:

I don't believe that she is genuinely interested in ideas in the

---

[1] Professor Milton Friedman, professor of economics, University of Chicago since 1948, Nobel prize winner for economics 1976 and author of (among others) *A Monetary History of the United States 1867–1960* (with Anna Schwartz) (1963); *Inflation: Causes and Consequence* (1963); *Price Theory* (1976).

[2] Friedrich von Hayek, economist and author of (among others) *The Road to Serfdom* (1944).

way that more profound people are. She came into politics with a very clear set of prejudices. One was about freedom, it was a misunderstanding of freedom. She came into politics opposed to organised labour, she came into politics opposed to state intervention and state spending and she now will grasp with great enthusiasm anybody who has ever given a lecture to the local Conservative Association on the vices of those things which she's always detested. I don't believe it is a mark of her intellectuality. I believe it is a mark of her desire to dress up her prejudices as if they were really opinions.

Whether opinions or prejudices, Thatcherism has been presented as a vision, and a rather grand one. It is the very vision, indeed, which has always troubled Tory traditionalists and prompted many a rebellion. If there is a leader of this faction, it is Francis Pym. He thinks the vision, even after six years, has not been widely shared:

Pym:

Yes, she certainly has that vision. But she's never actually been able to make it really exciting except for the people who understand the economic thinking behind it. A lot of people in the business world think a very, very great deal of it, but I'm talking about the great mass of people. I don't think it's been presented in a way that makes it really attractive or exciting to them, so that they feel that they, too, are involved on an expedition and an adventure to an exciting new world that they're all going to enjoy very much more than the last one.

The ideas which make up this vision have certainly not been a lifelong commitment. In Mrs Thatcher's years of uncomplaining servitude to Ted Heath's quite different economic policy, the prejudices may have been latent, but the opinions went unexpressed. More than anything it was a political accident, the fall of the Heath government in 1974, which made her stock her mind with something new. Before that she was simply not interested in much beyond the narrow world of the Department of Education where Sir William Pile was her senior civil servant.

Pile:

I think in the four years in the Department she showed, at all events, very little interest in anything outside the Department's brief, outside the contents of her red box. She devoured that, she mastered that down to the last statistic and the last comma, but anything outside the Department's range was not a matter she chose to discuss with us.

However, when Heath was defeated in 1974, she began to read her way towards some alternatives. This process was masterminded by a more political guru than those foreign economists, Sir Keith Joseph:

Joseph:

She was an avid reader. She is an avid reader. What I was able to do was to introduce her to some people and some writing that perhaps gave a framework to her own analysis.

But here we come up against a problem common to many politicians. How many of the books – whether by Friedman or Hayek or anyone else – did she actually read? If Joseph was her political mentor, Alfred Sherman, the founder-director of the Centre for Policy Studies, was her intellectual butler.

Sherman:

She read things that I brought her. I know that because she'd sometimes pick out a thing from memory two years later and quote it if necessary against you. So the stuff did pass through her mind.

This does not, however, make her an intellectual. Or if it does, it's only, according to another of her former advisers, Sir John Hoskyns, on the most cynical of definitions.

Hoskyns:

I don't think she is an intellectual type of person. She is inquisitive, she has a very inquiring mind, I think she feels she wants to know about everything. She would love, I'm sure, to have read every book that has ever been published. But I don't think that she is intellectual certainly in the sense that some prime ministers would like to be thought intellectual. If you take the Sherman definition of an intellectual, as 'a man who goes through the formality of reading the books he quotes from', she certainly reads the books she quotes from.

But Sir Alfred himself has few illusions. He still admires Mrs Thatcher, despite having been now thrust pretty firmly from the fold at No. 10. But he says that, in the ideas market, Mrs Thatcher is an entrepreneur and exploiter, not a creator of intellectual riches:

Sherman:

She's a consumer of ideas, she uses them, applies them. This is not unique, but rare, particularly in a Britain which in the last hundred years simply has developed an anti-intellectual tradition, and a philistinism. It didn't used to be so. In the Victorian age politicians were people of ideas; Disraeli, Gladstone, Peel,

Salisbury. The philistinism is a fairly recent development – it coincides with Britain's decline.

Arresting this decline is the purpose to which all these ideas, wherever they come from, are supposedly directed. One large idea – part economic and part political, with many offshoots – has driven her for ten years. Keith Joseph has no doubt that her personal commitment to this has been decisive: far more so than the partly accidental fact that the times seemed ready for it. And as its progenitor, he's the best person to put it into words:

Joseph:
She seems to me to have been gripped since before she won the leadership of the Tory party by a clear understanding, a passionately clear understanding, of the interacting causes of our relative economic decline. She saw it, as it seems to me, partly stemming from successive governments which by increasing the money supply kept on rescuing managements and labour from having to become more competitive. She saw it therefore as primarily a failure of government in creating the climate which enabled inefficiencies to continue to the point where all our neighbours soared past us in competitiveness, in prosperity, in social services, in standard of living and in purchasing power for all their people. She saw it infecting management which was allowed to be flabby. And she saw it as intensified or made worse and more difficult by the uncomprehending approach of trade unions who don't seem to realise where their members' interests lie.

When she got to No. 10, the acting-out of these truths became a complete and undeviating preoccupation. As far as the economic policy went, according to Sir Douglas Wass, whose lifetime in the Treasury gives him no fewer than ten administrations to compare her with, she became uniquely dominant.

Wass:
She is much more the First Lord of the Treasury than any previous holder of that office, at least that I'm aware of. She was after all a tax lawyer, she was the front bench spokesman in opposition for the Tory party,[1] and she'd made a considerable study of economic and financial policy in the course of the 1970s. Finally, I think she came into office feeling that economic recovery was crucial to the success of all other policies and therefore should command a very high priority on the

---

[1] From November 1974 to February 1975.

Prime Minister's work schedule. And she made a reality of that, there's no doubt that she was very, very concerned with the performance of the government's financial and economic policy, more so, I think, than any other prime minister I've worked for.

This immersion, however, did not drown her. The torrents of complex and confusing Treasury paper have not deadened her simple instincts. When Sir Alan Walters, an academic and a life-long British monetarist, became her economic adviser after eighteen months, the professor found the pupil still fully responsive:

Walters:

I am inclined to say she is a remarkable phenomenon. She has an instinctive understanding. Her instincts are for the most part accurate, good and very reliable, they are virtually always right. Sometimes they may be a little off, but as a rule she reacts instinctively correctly, more so, I think, than any other politician I've ever met. I must say she is one of the most splendid students. She was very quick and she asked most searching questions which as a teacher I've often wished for, but rarely seen and rarely heard.

But this is again a point on which there are two opinions. One man's brilliant and receptive student, asking all the right questions about economics, is another man's churner-out of scripted answers. The end-product is not necessarily wisdom, as Sir William Pile found at the Education Department a decade ago:

Pile:

It depends how you define wisdom, I suppose. If you mean that faced with unforeseen problems of conflicting natures that you haven't run into before, and where there's no rule of thumb to guide you, then the wise person will find a way of deciding the right course of action on the facts as they are in front of him or her. Now I didn't see any evidence of this. To every known set of problems she had a prefabricated answer. So I didn't think that wisdom of that kind was a pronounced characteristic. Clever is another word. The difference between being clever and wise is not an easy one, but there is a difference I think. She was clever in the sense that she was able to absorb an immense amount of information, she could recall it instantaneously, and she could articulate it, and use it and manage it with enormous efficiency. But this may have been, of course, the result of a competent ability to remember things, to recall things and did not, I think, necessarily prove that here was an enormously sophisticated intellectual mind. In brief I think she was a magnificent manager of information, a user of information. I do not think she ever showed an enormous intellectual brilliance in any field. And the wisdom that comes from having to make the right decision when there is nothing else to guide you is not something I noticed her possessing.

Neil Kinnock thinks roughly the same of her now: her cleverness is limited by her personal vision, which colours her judgement of intellect in others as well:

Kinnock:

Mrs Thatcher's appreciation of cleverness is directly related to the degree to which she happens to agree with the analysis offered by the clever person. Someone who is clever and would be recognised as being clever by any disinterested judge isn't recognised in Mrs Thatcher's book as having perception or a developed intellect – simply because she cannot bring herself to believe that anyone who radically disagrees with her has got the basic requirements of brightness, which are to see things with the clarity and simplicity with which she sees it. And that's a very selective view of intellect. She also, of course, doesn't seem to have much appreciation of the applied intellects, whether they manifest themselves in great cultural works, great artistic works or in works of rebellion against established wisdom. I don't think Mrs Thatcher is a cultured person in that sense. She's got what R. H. Tawney described as a sort of provincial preciousness that some people mistake for good taste and culture.[1] That is Tawney speaking, not me, but I think that if he'd known Margaret Thatcher he would have wanted to apply it to her.

Whatever qualities of mind Mrs Thatcher possesses, no one can doubt her skills in putting them over. To Peter Shore, she achieves one of the politician's most elusive objectives: saying for people what they have not quite got around to saying for themselves.

Shore:

She is undoubtedly a most formidable communicator. She has

---

[1] R. H. Tawney, *Equality*, Chapter Two, 'Inequality and Social Structure'; 'Culture may be fastidious, but fastidiousness is not culture; and, though vulgarity is an enemy of "reasonableness and a sense of values", it is less deadly an enemy than gentility and complacency. A cloistered and secluded refinement, intolerant of the heat and dust of creative effort, is the note not of civilization, but of the epochs which have despaired of it.'

the ability to take hold of complex issues and, if you like, simplify them, moralise them, according to her own bourgeois values, and to get them across. She's used it at every platform I've seen her on, from the House of Commons to a party conference, and above all on television and radio. Secondly, I think that she's sensed some of the kinds of moral considerations in politics that underlie people's political and economic attitudes, and I think she has articulated right-wing moral convictions in a more formidable and more committed way than any leader of the right in post-war Britain.

Clarity is the word which encapsulates this. Again and again people refer to it. It was the overwhelming majority choice among the politicians we asked to identify Mrs Thatcher's most distinguishing characteristic. It was, says former minister David Howell, the quality the Tories, when they elected her originally, wanted more than any other:

Howell:

One has to realise that there existed throughout the Conservative party in the late '70s – and Mrs Thatcher merely embodied this particularly crisply – a view that there had been too many deals with the trade unions and other figures behind closed doors and that things were not out in the open. In that sense there was a lack of clarity about national policy, too much corporatism and extra-parliamentary power broking. Mrs Thatcher stood very clearly and admirably against all this.

But she went further.

Howell:

It's in her character to impose precision and clarity on every situation. Well, situations aren't like that, they sometimes come up and hit you on the head and they're often very grey and complicated. So that creates a certain tension, a certain embattled sense at all times. I also feel the question of gender does come into this a bit, that Mrs Thatcher does regard a great many men as 'old women' sitting around in the Athenaeum or somewhere, fudging and nudging and compromising while the ship of state sinks, and she wasn't having any of that.

The clarity of her opinions, and the fierceness of her commitment to them, were put most severely to the test as she approached the end of her second year in power. This was the moment when the Heath government had performed its U-turn away from financial stringency. As 1980 unfolded, she came under steady pressure to do the same: relax spending targets and soften fiscal discipline.

Sir John Hosykns recalls the pledge she made to resist it:

Hosykns:

In the middle of 1980 when unemployment was already rising fast, bankruptcies were rising, and it was obviously all getting pretty hairy, I and one or two other advisers went to her and asked, 'If there is ever going to be any sort of U-turn on policy you absolutely must think about it now.' It had obviously worried me because it had so often happened before that if people kept saying 'no, no, no', they ended up saying 'yes'. We wanted to be absolutely sure that if, in fact, privately there was a view in her mind – or in that of any of her colleagues – that there might have to be any significant change in policy, one really had to start preparing the ground for it, rather than be made to look utterly idiotic at the last minute. She simply said, 'You know, I would rather go down than do that, so forget it.' And I just remember saying, 'Thank you very much, because we now know exactly where we stand and I think you are absolutely right.' There was very impressive readiness to look right through to the end and say, 'That is what we'll do.'

The 1981 budget, the end-product of this pledge, was the high-water mark of Thatcherism: the moment when, against all the advice of the more conventional Conservatives, Mrs Thatcher and her Chancellor, Sir Geoffrey Howe, constructed a highly restrictive budget, which, in their opinion, became the base on which all subsequent success has rested. A key figure in the battle to push the budget through was her newly-installed economic adviser Sir Alan Walters, whom she had just taken on as a full-time personal economic adviser.

Walters:

In my judgement the government really had to wrench their policy on to course and they had to establish that. We were not going to go forward with enormous unsupportable borrowings again. We were going to convince the financial markets that we were in truth a reforming government, and we were going to get inflation down and we were going to get borrowing down. I think this course reinforced Mrs Thatcher's basic policy beliefs and I think it was rather useful for her to have someone like me to talk to about this major decision. Of course the majority of people, including some in the civil service and certainly some in the House of Commons, believed that we should have a much softer budget. Indeed 364 economists

wrote saying that we should have had a softer budget.[1] But I
believed that it was very important that we establish the
credibility of that policy and the consistency of that policy, and
of course I think in retrospect that this has been shown to be
right – from mid-1981 we started the recovery in output and we
haven't really looked back since.

Walters regarded even the Treasury, that temple of fiscal rigour,
as in need of being shored up.

Walters:

I don't think it is difficult to see why. The Treasury is very
much influenced by the political situation and they were
reading the political situation as being dangerous because
unemployment was increasing – and of course their standard
reaction over the years has been when unemployment is
increasing we must increase the budget deficit, we must inject
money into the system. Those latent ideas always tend to
surface and, even though they are trying to put through a
reform, they say, 'Well, we can't do it this year, alas. Let's do it
next year when things are better, or the year after.' And I think
it is entirely understandable, but at the time I took a very tough
line on it because it seemed to me if we didn't have the type of
budget we did eventually get in 1981 – a very tough one indeed
– then we would have a financial crisis on our hands.

Interestingly, John Hoskyns, looking back, suspects that the 1981
budget may have been too severely restrictive. But it registered a
great political investment.

Hoskyns:

I'm not absolutely sure with hindsight that we might not have
been able to sneak by with a slightly looser budget than we
had, but the point is that the down side of trying to sneak by
like that and getting it wrong would have been absolutely
horrendous, so as a matter of risk analysis it was important
to take out all the insurance one could. That was the view
Geoffrey Howe took and I thought it was a very courageous
view. I don't think there was ever any question of her saying, 'Oh well, it is politically impossible.' She said, 'It has got to
be done. I'll back you.'

So vigorous thrift is the first pillar of her economic attitudes. But it
is not the most famous. For this we must summon up the picture
of the good housekeeper, the Grantham grocer's daughter, the

---

[1] On 30 March 1981.

prime minister who really does believe that the thrifty principles of home management are a perfectly sufficient guide to the management of the national economy. Lord Harris of High Cross, founder of the Institute of Economic Affairs and a polemicist at whose feet she once sat, portrays her as a kind of supreme housewife to the nation:

Harris:
The central escape that politicians have made is that the issues of government are totally different from the ordinary issues of housekeeping, and of balancing books and of counting the change. I was shocked in the House of Lords to see the way in which Bills and proposals involving hundreds of millions of pounds are discussed quite differently from the way in which any group that I'm involved in as a trustee spends a few hundred pounds or a few thousand pounds, where a quite different degree of involvement and intensity of argument is applied. So I quite like the way that she regards it all as her money. She sometimes talks about *my* industries and *my* budget. I quite like that, actually.

This has been a brilliant communications triumph – for which pupil gets full marks even from sophisticated professor.

Walters:
The jibe that she's developed economics from considering household decisions seems to me to be an accolade. I mean, this is how you should think about economics, you should think concretely. She thinks in household terms to work out a principle, and she works it out so that it is consistent with her observations and consistent with her experience – very valuable.

Such simplicities, however, don't satisfy everybody. Good housekeeping may sound like good politics, and even good morality, but Roy Jenkins, a former Chancellor of the Exchequer, says it's lousy economics:

Jenkins:
It's good populist stuff, it sounds simple, it sounds good and irrefutable, but I think it is nonsense because there is an essential difference between the position of a family budget and a national budget. And that is that on the whole, a family cannot increase its income by increasing its spending. Whereas a nation, a government, by increasing its spending, not by doing it indiscriminately, but by doing it wisely, by well-directed investment spending, can substantially increase the

total of the national income. And therefore it is one of these simple analogies which sounds splendid, but is in fact deeply misleading.

Her own first Chancellor, Sir Geoffrey Howe, feels that such criticisms are quite misplaced:

Howe:

Politicians have a hapless task, don't they? On the one hand they're in danger of being denounced for failing to achieve clarity, failing to get their message through, and then when someone achieves a dramatic success in communication – as undoubtedly Mrs Thatcher has done – they get accused of over-simplification. I think that most people find the understanding of economic affairs profoundly difficult. It is in fact necessary to go back to very elementary principles if you're to begin getting across a very simple case. And that's what she's done with some success.

This is accepted even by some of her enemies. Michael Meacher, MP, on the Labour left, acknowledges the effectiveness of a message he profoundly disagrees with:

Meacher:

She carves out a single phrase, a sentence, two sentences which convey a very powerful message that more often than not strikes a chord, even though I think it is sometimes quite wrong. I think in particular she's suggested that you can't run a country which lives beyond its means just like you can't run a family that runs beyond its means. The truth is that of course you can't overspend as a family or as a household, but it is an absurd analogy to suggest that you can't do that as a country. The fact is countries and above all companies invest in the future, they borrow to invest in a bigger future, and that's perfectly normal economics. But she has got people to accept contraction by this analogy with household economics.

To a businessman like Sir Monty Finniston, on the other hand, the obsession with household economics is also an error. He was Chairman of British Steel from 1973–6, and senses a large gap between the business mind and this prime minister's:

Finniston:

The fact that she's got a Victorian ethical standard with regard to thrift and other matters suggests to me that she confuses home economics with business economics. The two are quite different. They are different in scale and they are different in techniques and they are different in methods. I mean you

don't have overdrafts and loans and equity when you're running your home and you don't commit yourself to resources
and risks in the home that you do in business.

According to her colleague and critic, Peter Walker, Mrs Thatcher
has in fact modified some of her simple ideas. As the only wet still
in the Cabinet, he may be a slightly suspect source. But he looks
at British Leyland – for years a massive drain on anyone's household budget – and sees evidence that the rigours of theoretical
Thatcherism have succumbed to the political logic of people like
himself:

Walker:

Under any sort of free market force doctrine British Leyland
would have been allowed to disappear, and would have gone
to the wall very quickly. But she and the Cabinet were in total
agreement that the disastrous effect of that on the economics of
the Midlands, on unemployment, on the balance of trade, was
such that you had to go and pour vast sums of public expenditure in to see that it was rescued and saved.[1] And so I think the
purist doctrines that you can enjoy when you're in opposition,
when you don't have the responsibilities of government, look
different when you have to take the practical decisions. I think
perhaps one of the problems is that the rhetoric is often
different from the performance. And I'm glad to say that quite
often the performance is better than the rhetoric.

Not perhaps what every smaller company bankrupted in the last
six years would say. But here we touch on the second distinctive
element of the ideas and prejudices Mrs Thatcher has synthes-
ised into an economic policy. If housekeepers are the model for
thrift, entrepreneurs are the model for growth. Places like BL,
although they have been preserved, are in fact the antithesis of
the kind of business she really believes in. Sir Monty Finniston
feels that size was only one factor in this prejudice:

Finniston:

I don't think the size worried her over much. After all she likes
ICI. You can't say that she dislikes size as such. What she likes
is success. And the world has its successes but it also has its
failures. She doesn't like failures and unfortunately in business you have failures. After all we've got over a thousand

---

[1] In 1975, the majority of the shares of British Leyland had been acquired by
the Labour government. In January 1981 the Conservative government
agreed to invest an additional £990 million in the company over a period of
two years to prevent it going bankrupt.

bankruptcies a month, and have had for three years now.[1]
And for all the small businesses that start, the death rate is fantastically high.

To her most dedicated allies, like Norman Tebbit, the fact that more small businesses than ever before have gone down in the last six years confirms rather than vitiates her instinct:

Tebbit:

Life should never be safe for entrepreneurs. If you make life safe for entrepreneurs they begin to behave like heads of nationalised industries or civil servants. Now civil servants and heads of nationalised industries are important people with qualities of their own. But they're different to entrepreneurs. Entrepreneurs have to have life unsafe. That's the very quality of entrepreneurship. But she has certainly made the country safer for entrepreneurs.

Finniston thinks that she herself might make a good entrepreneur:

Finniston:

Yes, she takes risks, the Falklands was a risk. And her attitude to other things has been risky. She might well be a good entrepreneur. And, yes, she is sufficiently – I was going to use the word obstinate but perhaps that's too strong a word – she's sufficiently committed to see the end of the affair. She doesn't give up very easily. Yes, she might make a good entrepreneur.

But he disagrees with Norman Tebbit that her government has made life safer for them:

Finniston:

It's certainly not made it any safer because I don't think the intervention of the government in the affairs of business has changed the economy of this country one iota. I think we're still facing, as a country, international competition in manufacturing products, and in services for that matter, but products in particular, in which the government has had no way of modifying the direction in which we go. We've never had an industrial policy in this country. If she says, I've got nothing to do with business and I'm going to remain out, then she can't claim anything for either the failures or for the successes. One must ask, 'Has she made a positive contribution?' And the answer is she hasn't. The budgets over the past five years have

---

[1] From July 1983 – July 1985 the average number of company liquidations was just over 1000 a month. *British Business*, HMSO, 26 July 1985.

made little if any difference at all. I mean there have been trivial peripheral activities, but whether it's the Business Expansion Scheme or whether it's corporation tax or national insurance surcharge, they've made very little difference. It hasn't influenced business at all. People haven't said, 'Oh, now that she's taken this off, or the Chancellor's done this, I must re-look at my capital investment programme.' It doesn't happen at all. The things that she does believe in are, as far as businesses are concerned, marginal. And what makes them worse, they are not only marginal, they depend upon random forces. Free market forces are a random force. And I don't believe in running my life and the life of a country randomly. I like to know where I am going even if I fail.

But it's not just a matter of the free market. Sheer romantic idolatry comes with it as well. Comparing herself with a successful businessman, Mrs Thatcher can exhibit, uncharacteristically, something of the awed humility expressed here by Sir Geoffrey Howe:

Howe:

When one encounters someone who has created a business, starting with £100 capital and two employees twenty-five years ago, which is now employing tens of thousands of people with a huge turnover, having created a completely new enterprise, one's bound to look at it and say, 'Well, has my achievement been comparable to that?'

And this feeling is reflected in the way the prime minister disposes of the patronage at her personal disposal, as Norman Tebbit has noticed:

Tebbit:

She's certainly done a great deal to help entrepreneurs, not least by her attitude towards them. The receptions at No. 10 for entrepreneurs and for people in entrepreneurial industries are a mark of that. She's always taken a close interest in who gets recommended or who is recommended for honours from the world of industry and commerce. And I think she's happier when she sees the entrepreneurial spirit being rewarded than when everything goes to the great and the good of industry.

Now such bonuses are all very well, and they send out clear signals. Entrepreneurs are undoubtedly in favour – and have had scores of legislative advantages conferred on them. But is there, here again, more talk than results, more atmospherics than real advance? Entrepreneurs live in an economic as well as a rhetorical climate. As Peter Shore says, whether you're big or little, efficiency cannot be the only lifeline:

Shore:

There are many industries you can point to and say, 'Clearly their productivity has improved, yes.' But in attempting to deal with that problem, she also switched off demand in the economy, and the result has been that we may have in certain truncated industries more output per head, greater efficiency as it were, but the loss of the rest has been simply phenomenal, and the total is down. It isn't that the efficient units have grown and the inefficient units have been cut out, it is that the efficient units have just been sustained and the greater part of the industry, I'm thinking of steel for example, but I could think of others too, have just been wiped out.

Or there comes a time when the results have to be counted. Where Peter Walker expressed mordant relief that the performance was better than the rhetoric, Roy Jenkins thinks there's nothing to choose between them:

Jenkins:

What I think she's done is to create an atmosphere of a sort of Rotary Club culture in which it's felt that small businessmen are the most desirable people in the country. But in fact, if judged by the hard standards in which they have to operate, she's made the climate much more difficult. There've never been more small businessmen going bankrupt and it's never in many ways been more difficult to get going. The rhetoric is that she's enormously improved the performance of the economy and in particular the performance of small businesses, whereas the reality is that although she's diagnosed certain evils, so far from curing them, in fact, judged by every material standard, she's made things worse over the past five years.

But before that assessment is written in stone, the third element of her personal agenda must be laid out. She's pro-thrift and pro-business – but anti-union. A direct and unvarnished description, and one to which no professional politician is ever willing to admit. In Mrs Thatcher's case, however, we have good evidence for its truth from Jim Prior, the man who had to reconcile it with his own more pragmatic view, as the Conservative party's employment spokesman for more than half the Thatcher years:

Prior:

I think that Margaret always loathed the trade unions and she loathed the closed shop in particular, and she was very wrapped up in the personal freedom aspects that she felt the unions were seeking to deny.

This presiding conviction did not derive from any intimate acquaintance with the people who run trade unions.

Prior:

I don't think she knew trade union leaders at all well. She knew Frank Chapple a bit, but she relied I think very greatly on Woodrow Wyatt to keep her in touch with trade union opinion. I can think of more reliable sources of information than Woodrow Wyatt,[1] but he was, as it were, her secret weapon which she trotted out from time to time without ever mentioning his name. And I think other than that there were no trade union leaders she had any contact with except on one occasion we did meet them all round the table, Jack Jones and Hughie Scanlon and Basnett and Len Murray and so on.[2] But she really never got to know trades union leaders at all; I don't think she knows them now.

There developed, therefore, a conflict: one which is quite typical of the Thatcher style – also very visible in foreign policy – whereby the Prime Minister's instincts are resisted by the departmental minister in charge, with more or less public displays of disloyalty, on occasion, on each side.

Prior:

I was saying, 'Look, for goodness sake, take it easy. There are many things we can do if we do them slowly and we do them steadily, and do it a step by step approach.' And of course the *Daily Express* and the *Daily Mail* and the *Daily Telegraph* were all vying for blood. They always want people's blood as long as it's not their own, and they wanted much more vicious legislation than we introduced.

The Prime Minister did, however, learn.

Prior:

We held the line. And in many ways she has told me since that she's been quite grateful that we did hold the line and that we didn't go mad on trades union legislation at that time.

---

[1] Sir Woodrow Wyatt, newspaper columnist and Labour MP from 1945–55 and 1959–70, left the Labour party in 1976. He was knighted by Mrs Thatcher in 1983.
[2] Jack Jones, General Secretary T&GWU 1969–78;
Hugh Scanlon (now Lord Scanlon), President AUEW 1968–78;
David Basnett, General Secretary GMWU 1973–82 and GMBATU 1982–5;
Len Murray (now Lord Murray), General Secretary of the TUC, 1973–84.

A verdict, it seems, which is also endorsed by Mr Prior's immediate successor, Norman Tebbit – the very vessel of purest Thatcherism, but showing that it can be diluted:

Tebbit:

The costs were there, the great shouting matches and the yells and the kill the bill campaigns and all the essential divisiveness, but now one sees the strength of that legislation beginning to show.[1] It's not perfect. The way it is used isn't perfect. But it had a very significant effect, for example, in the last twelve months of the coal strike.[2]

Peter Shore agrees that the effect has been significant, but thinks that other factors have helped weaken the unions.

Shore:

One is the great increase in unemployment. I think this has always been one of the things in the back of her mind. As far as Mrs Thatcher is concerned, unemployment is a mixed evil because with three million unemployed, it has changed the balance of power in British industry and in the British economy. At the same time, of course, she's introduced a whole series of small but increasingly effective cumulative measures which really will inhibit trade union power.

The crushing of union power is one effect of the idea called Thatcherism. It is fairly precise and quite indisputable. There is another in the same class: the outcome of the privatisation policy, as David Howell describes it:

Howell:

Remember that she's taken up the theme of the redistribution of capital in a way that makes Tony Benn look like a moderate. Mrs Thatcher has embraced the theme and dream that we should have an irreversible widespread ownership of assets and capital in the nation and that this in a sense was the antidote to British socialism.[3]

Indeed, she never saw nationalisation as, in any true sense, ownership by the public. She had always had a poor view of nationalised industry chairmen. An encounter with them shortly after she had become leader of the opposition showed her mettle,

---

[1] *Employment Act*, 1980; *Employment Act*, 1982; *Trades Union Act*, 1984.

[2] The strike involving NUM members in the majority of the coalfields lasted from March 1984 to March 1985.

[3] For example, British Telecom floated £3900 million worth of shares on the Stock Exchange on 20 November 1984, offering 50.2% of the state-owned company for sale.

as Monty Finniston, then Chairman of British Steel, remembers:

Finniston:

In a way it was a precursor to her attitude towards the National Union of Mineworkers. She virtually roasted poor Derek Ezra alive.[1] Every time you mention the occasion to him he goes white. And it really was a most extraordinary affair. She said that, when she got into power, he wouldn't get away with what he was doing in the Coal Board with the miners, she'd see to that. That was virtually the tenor of her case, and it was only the intervention of Peter Thorneycroft,[2] Richard Marsh[3] and in a small part myself that prevented a fracas.

The question, however, is where all these prejudices and certainties have got us? Privatisation, like everything else, is only a means to the end of greater prosperity. To Neil Kinnock, it is also only a sideshow to the larger story of continual national decline:

Kinnock:

The context has been changed by the scale of industrial devastation, particularly in the manufacturing industries. It means that our base for future economic development is eroded, especially as the oil revenues run down, and the oil runs out. Now that's the extent of change that has taken place. Efficiency, unit cost productivity, our competitiveness in the world, have all been retarded, so that the consequence of the application of what's become known as Thatcherism, with all its lauding of profit and cost reduction, and thinning down and making more efficient, actually isn't borne out by the facts in terms of the British economy generally, and manufacturing industry in particular. Even worse, there are erosions of our training base, our research and development base, which mean that redevelopment in the future is going to be somewhat more difficult because of the scale of the reduction over the last six or seven years – possibly eight or nine years by that time.

On the other hand, Thatcherism was an idea whose time turned out, in some respects, to have come. Even its critics admit as much. When Chris Patten, now Minister of State at the Department of Education, ran the Tory research department ten years ago, he thought the blueprint of the far Right was a non-starter:

---

[1] Sir Derek Ezra (now Lord Ezra) was Chairman of the National Coal Board 1971–82;
[2] Lord Thorneycroft was Chairman of the Conservative party 1975–81;
[3] Sir Richard Marsh (now Lord Marsh) was Chairman of British Railways Board 1971–6.

Patten:

I always thought it was both impossible and wrong to change what had been conceived of as the middle ground intellectually and politically in our political argument. If you look at the way we've managed the economy previously – demand management, incomes policy and so on, I'd always thought that you couldn't shift polite opinion on those sort of issues. Well, she shifted it. And we're now in a position in which even some of her sternest critics, at least in other parties, find themselves having to ape some of her attitudes. David Owen does it, even Mr Kinnock does it occasionally.

Jim Prior agrees that he and his friends made what was, in the short term, a mistaken political judgement:

Prior:

I think our judgement proved false to the extent that many of us thought that the social consequences of three million unemployed, let alone the political consequences of three million unemployed, were unacceptable, and that therefore an economic policy which was going to have that sort of effect in the short run, whatever it might say about the long run, was doomed to failure because it would simply not be acceptable, and we would be swept out of office by one thing or another. And so to that extent I think we were wrong.

But vindication may not be far away.

Prior:

Where I think we were absolutely right was in our belief that the policy itself would not work, and I think it's abundantly clear that reliance on the sort of tight fiscal policy that we've had at a time of world recession, together with adherence to a theory – at any rate in the early years of the government – of monetary policy, has simply not produced a prosperity, not produced a growth, and has seen Britain decline further in relation to its competitors rather than improve. So to that extent I think we were wrong about the social and political implications of the policy but right about the economic policy itself.

On that policy, the jury is still out. After the bad years, some things were better. Inflation came down from over 20% to under 7%. There was growth for five years. Industry, what was left of it, was obliged to function far more efficiently. There remains, however, the overarching fact of unemployment. At over three and a quarter million in the autumn of 1985, this has more than doubled since 1979. The government's objective is surely to run the economy at a high level of activity while achieving both low inflation and low unemployment. After nearly seven years, it cannot be long before its failure to have done this becomes a major political liability. Peter Shore, and his Labour colleagues, are standing on the side-lines waiting to capitalise on it:

Shore:

I'm not an over-optimistic person about the British economy, because you can't be optimistic after many years of experience and study, but if you'd asked me if I genuinely thought that the '80s were going to be the British decade, I would have said 'yes'. And it hasn't been. It's been absolutely terrible. Mrs Thatcher began after all with the – in a sense very appealing – self-proclaimed objective of ending Britain's relative economic decline since the war, and putting us back into the ranks of the high-growth countries. And in her first four years she actually achieved not relative economic decline, but absolute economic decline. At the end of the first four years of Mrs Thatcher, in spite of the massive outpouring of North Sea oil wealth, we are a poorer country. I don't mean that necessarily in terms of distribution of wealth – another matter entirely – but the national wealth and product was actually lower four years after she came in than it was when she took over.

Would Norman Tebbit claim that six years is too early to make the reckoning?

Tebbit:

Yes, I think so. And therefore there is a good deal of faith still involved. But a damn sight less faith than you would need to believe that the right way forward would be to centralise the command of the economy and to go back to either the Morrisonian[1] concept of nationalisation, or the Wilson-Callaghan concept of exchange control and internal regulation and social contract.

Francis Pym and the other Tory critics don't want to get back to that either. But Mr Pym still believes that the balance of the policy is mistaken. Having come to power with a great idea called Thatcherism, Mrs Thatcher would not revise it when the world plunged into recession, very soon after the 1979 election.

---

[1] Herbert Morrison, a Labour minister from 1929–31 and 1945–51 and deputy leader of the Labour party, gave his name to the form of nationalisation which is based on the idea of a public corporation. The government should set broad objectives and appoint the Board but should not be involved in day-to-day management; it should operate on an arm's-length and hands-off basis.

Pym:

And that meant that the economic rewards of the policy put forward were going to be very long delayed. I think it would have been right to tell people of that right away instead of doing what the Prime Minister and the government decided to do, which was to go on pretending that the only thing to do was to follow our economic policy and all will come right in the end. And I think her view on unemployment has been that it is very unfortunate that unemployment went up, but the only thing to do is to get down inflation, to have a rigid economic policy called monetarism – not pure monetarism but monetarism as it came to be known – and if that happened with a better working economy and so forth, all the jobs would come back. That is the pretence that has gone on ever since, and I was a critic of that in government, and I have been a passionate critic of it ever since, because I think it's misleading people. The world is different. No, I think she thought that, by imposing this monetarism on the country and sticking rigidly to it, and making sure her Chancellor stuck rigidly to it, no matter how many factories close, and no matter what happens it will all come right in the end. I think that's what she thought, but I would be very, very surprised if she thought that today.

Francis Pym said this well before the nadir of the government's popularity, in the summer of 1985, and before the strategic economic judgements – as between rigour and laxity, between the merits of tax cuts and public spending – were fixed as a prelude to Mrs Thatcher's third general election. Ceaseless debate attended these judgements, with the minutest examination of the government's words and actions. The language of ministers softened slightly and, compared with the heady rigour of the early years, some of the figures began to be fudged. But essentially Mr Pym has been proved wrong. Mrs Thatcher's policy has not changed course or lost the optimism underlying it – as the continuing discontent of the Pymite faction, it nothing else, very clearly shows.

'Where there is Discord may we Bring Harmony'

First Broadcast: 26 May 1985

It has been a matter of frequent remark that when Mrs Thatcher's party was elected to power in May 1979, she paused on the threshold of 10, Downing Street to utter the prayer of St Francis: 'Where there is discord, may we bring harmony; where there is error, may we bring truth; where there is doubt, may we bring faith; where there is despair, may we bring hope.' It has also been observed that there appears to be some discrepancy between those imprecations and the sentiments seemingly revealed by the policies the Thatcher government has pursued. The purpose of this chapter is to explore one of the most contradictory dimensions of the Thatcher phenomenon: her belief in God – or at any rate St Francis – and her simultaneous belief in Mammon as the deity that really presides over how society does and should work.

Michael Meacher is a Labour politician: the most eloquent of that quite substantial school on the left which thinks Mrs Thatcher is wonderful – but not for her Franciscan virtues:

Meacher:
Personally I think that she has the qualities of a very great politician. I believe she has tremendous conviction, she has drive, she has commitment, she is totally genuine. On the other side I think she has a certain tunnel vision, she is uncompromising, she goes over the top too much – she did over the miners, she tried to make out that Arthur Scargill was Galtieri[1] and that the miners were the Argies. I think that view does not go down well in the country. And I think she's deeply lacking in compassion and sensitivity, and for all the attempt of her creators to try and induce that feeling of sincerity – the careful way they manicure the hair, the eyebrows, the voice, and the intonation – she has really become a professional actress in so many ways that I think those qualities don't come over.

Immediately, however, we are presented with a paradox. What-

---

[1] Arthur Scargill, President of the National Union of Mineworkers 1982–; General Galtieri, President of Argentina Dec 1981–June 1982.

ever the truth about her attitude to policy – how she would reconcile unemployment, social division, inner-city collapse and all the rest of it, with the harmony and hope St Francis prayed for – at one level she is the very model of a caring person.

Du Cann:

I could produce for you now, out of my own experience, a dozen hand-written letters that I've had from her at various times. The night of the election for the 1922 Committee I went out to dinner with my wife and we had a very good dinner with some old friends and we got back to our flat at about half past ten at night – and on the floor of our flat was a hand-written letter from the Prime Minister. Now there is an example of thoughtfulness for you.

That was a letter commiserating with Sir Edward du Cann hours after he'd been voted out of the chairmanship of the 1922 Committee of Tory backbenchers after 12 years, in November 1984. There have been numerous others, to people she has never met. Ian Gow, parliamentary private secretary and general factotum from 1979 to 1983, remembers one of the bloodiest moments in Ulster, five years earlier in August 1979:

Gow:

After the tragedy at Warrenpoint when seventeen of our soldiers were killed, the Prime Minister sat down straight away and wrote seventeen letters, one to each of those widows.

Such proofs of humanity express, Gow insists, Margaret Thatcher's true nature:

Gow:

Her capacity to feel affection for people in distress, her capacity to feel affection for her friends, was something which they understood and which I understood but which the world doesn't seem yet to understand.

The closer you are, it seems, the more irresistibly selfless is the personality you come in contact with. Former Party Chairman John Gummer was pretty close:

Gummer:

When she was leader of the opposition, if any of us were doing anything to help in the office working on statements, speeches and that sort of thing, I've never known anyone who was as concerned as she was to see that you were looked after, that somebody had organised your getting home in the middle of the night or your getting some food, before she was the slightest bit interested in herself. She's not somebody who is interested in her own comfort and she can put in long hours of work without food and drink, but she is terribly concerned about other people. She remembers other people's family circumstances too, never fails to be interested, and to show that she's interested – not just in a kind of polite politician's way, but in a very real sense and in very personal terms. Nor are these proofs of humanity confined to the small change of political life. There are the consistent courtesies few prime ministers – especially perhaps male ones – have time for. Reg Prentice, who left the Labour party to join the Conservatives in 1977, found to his surprise that the Prime Minister took a close personal interest in the arrangements for his crossing the floor of the House, an interest which went beyond that of a party leader celebrating a substantial political coup:

Prentice:
I found that she was extremely concerned that the situation should not be more uncomfortable for me than it had to be, and she took great care of the details. She was concerned with which day I would come into the Commons for the first time to sit on the Conservative benches. That was fairly easy to predict because I actually changed parties during the recess, so it was going to be the day after we came back.[1] Then she was concerned that the Conservative whips should organise some Members to be there and she asked me which row I would go and sit in so that there would be a number of them there and they could give a cheer as I came in. I think her first concern was that politically the situation should be carried off well, but she was also concerned for me personally.

Lord Whitelaw has observed that in all matters relating to individuals the lady is somewhat less than iron:

Whitelaw:
I think possibly she feels herself more vulnerable when she's dealing with some rather tricky personal issue. I don't think any leader likes personal difficulties. No leader likes changes in their government, getting rid of old friends, dealing with some of the appalling personal problems every leader has to face. She doesn't like those at all. But perhaps that is when she is very much human, much to be admired, but of course at the same time, like every human being, vulnerable.

---

[1] 3 November 1977.

All of which cuts very little ice with the representatives of the wide world outside the privately sensitive, even tearful, salons of the entourage. Neil Kinnock, Labour's leader, has analysed the contrast between her private and public behaviour:

Kinnock:

Mrs Thatcher has a great sense of propriety and she believes, as many women from her particular class believe, and certainly women with important positions believe, that it's part of their duty to be solicitous and kindly in that official way, and she is fastidious in following that through. It doesn't mean however that there is a depth of passion about injustice or individuals' lack of advantage. Mrs Thatcher is characteristically given to blaming people for their own misfortune to an extent which is very unusual amongst modern politicians of any political party or any political persuasion. And that I think explains the divergence between the courteous private individual and holder of important office, and the abrupt and apparently soulless public individual who's got very little time for those who come at the back of any queue.

Roy Hattersley, his deputy, finds this divergence explicable but not impressive:

Hattersley:

Mrs Thatcher may write notes when she hears that her collea-gues are ill, she may actually genuinely worry about her sick staff, but at the same time she is responsible for policies which are causing enormous suffering and enormous hardship. Mrs Thatcher has ended the public sector house-building pro-gramme which means that thousands of families will live in squalor for the next five years, rather than live in decent houses. Now in the great balance I think this more than out-weighs a letter to a secretary saying, 'I'm sorry you had flu last week.' If we are judging Mrs Thatcher by the concern she shows, her policies show an enormous lack of concern, and I don't think there is any inconsistency between that and going through the social graces of being polite when she hears about sickness or bereavement.

Social concern is what we're talking about, and at one level there's no doubt Mrs Thatcher experiences it. She is deeply bothered about 'society'. Nobody with her missionary sense of self-belief – occasionally known as hubris – could be accused of having an underdeveloped sense of social purpose. She really believes British society can be changed, and that she's the person to do it. This involves her, however, in taking the unorthodox political stance of rejecting soft soap and soothing language. We must explore what her view is, in all its harshness, and look at the devices she has used to mitigate and deflect the political damage such harshness would normally bring with it.

John Gummer thinks all she is being is honest:

Gummer:

There is nothing that annoys her more than those who want to sound good and sound pious about unemployment but will not pay the price. That is a part of her absolute fascination with the need to tell the truth, because in her analysis of what has been wrong in Britain, people have bought votes on the compassion argument, when what they've really done is to be hypocritical. They've not been prepared to say, 'Well, the cost of this, if we're actually going to do it, means that those in work must not allow their wages to rise.' Now if you believe that, you've actually got to be very tough on it.

And being tough, Gummer believes, means choosing which is the really urgent part of your message.

Gummer:

In a society which has gone down the sentimental road, where compassion has become a sort of code-word for inaction, you can't show all facets of your character. You're bound to show whichever part of your character is needed at the time, and what was needed at the time when she came to power, and what is needed now, is a change in the atmosphere and the attitude of Britain to a lot of hard things. What she feels absolutely dedicated to is that if you are going to do the things for the developing countries or for the poor or for any section of the population about which she cares, then you've got to be tough enough to achieve the kind of society which can deliver the economic goods. That means she's got to go on talking about the need to pay our way, the boringness of the fact that if you don't earn enough then you can't spend money on things that really matter. That must show that harder side of her.

Norman Tebbit, probably the nearest thing she has to an alter ego in the Cabinet, denies that this attitude alienates her from ordinary people, or puts her only on the side of the successful:

Tebbit:

What she perceives is the fact that just those ordinary people, as you put them, the chap who pays his income tax and works his forty odd hours a week, is crucially dependent upon how successful the successful are. And therefore it's in the interest of the ordinary people, for want of a better expression, that we encourage and drive forward the successful, because they're the mainspring of the economy and it's by their abilities that the wealth-creating potential of the others will be brought out and will be harnessed.

If this means ditching the usual rhetoric of social concern for the under-privileged, Tebbit finds the necessary rationalisation for it:

Tebbit:

I think one is speaking to and for the under-privileged in the drive to improve our ability to create wealth in the country. One can go and talk to and for the under-privileged endlessly, but unless you've got the resources to change their state, it's just wind, isn't it? And the Prime Minister's feeling is that we've had far, far too much of that wind in the past. What we actually need is to create the means with which to do something about all the ills that so many people complain of.

In other words: forget about compassion, that buzzword of the '70s. Oddly enough, as an analytical statement, there's a certain similarity of perception between Norman Tebbit and Neil Kinnock.

Kinnock:

I think compassion is the major virtue of the strong. And I think to apply compassion in an organised fashion which will ensure that the purposes of it reach the targets is probably the toughest option of all, especially in a democracy where there are all kinds of other inhibitions and disruptions and difficulties in economic terms. What we are seeing now, of course, is the reassertion of the values of compassion, not out of any softness or soppiness or oversentimentality, but because people are again realising that this country works better when it works together, and Mrs Thatcher very clearly and very deliberately is a divisive force. I don't think that she'd want to claim anything else, she actually does believe that Britain must be led in new directions by first emaciating it and then rebuilding it.

Government ministers use the same kind of metaphor – but for them the slimming-down produces not emaciation but muscle, strength, an economy with the flab cut out of it. There, however, any agreement about what Mrs Thatcher really wants to do disappears. Professor Sir Alan Walters, formerly her economic adviser, pictures a politician not merely acting out the harsh equations of Tebbitland but creating an idyll of community life:

Walters:
Yes, there is a Britain she wants to see. It is based on solid family moral values. It is based on freedom, liberty, on responsibility, and also – this is important I think – it is not the sort of *laissez-faire* community of the ideologues of the left and the right. It is a community where of course people do things for the community. It is rather like the sort of ideal or idealised Victorian society where people did do a great deal of voluntary work for the community, and people were very upright and honest. I think that is the sort of view she takes of the good life.

Can this benign social reformer really be the same person Roy Hattersley is talking about?

Hattersley:
Mrs Thatcher is one of the most ruthless party politicians this country has ever seen and very clearly has a ruthless election strategy, which is to put together a coalition of people who have benefited materially from her administration. If you are in work, if you are not in the lower income groups in work, if you are not black, if you don't live in the north-east of England or central belt of Scotland, if you are not a pensioner or sick, you will probably have done materially rather better under five years of Thatcherism than you were doing when she was elected. And Mrs Thatcher's technique is to try and create 55% of the population who are in that position and hope that they will vote for her, ignoring the 45% whose conditions have deteriorated.

The truth is that such a person can co-exist with the prophet of communal harmony Alan Walters was portraying, but only if you accept one vital premise. This is that the new society shall harmonise itself around the values of property, of money, of success. Levelling up towards the successful rather than down towards the failures is the goal Mrs Thatcher has set this society. The coalition she wants to build is indeed of the non-poor, as Ian Gow makes very clear:

Gow:
She admires success. She wants to create conditions in which we can be a more successful Britain, but, of course, not everybody can succeed. She wants more and more people to succeed. Every man a capitalist, every man as successful as he or she can be. Everybody able to develop his and her talents. But at the end of the day she also understands that for those who are not able to provide for themselves, then there must be proper provision by the state.

85

And the millions who will never be, in her terms, successful capitalists?

Gow:

But more and more people are becoming capitalists. Wealth is being spread ever more widely. 63% of our fellow country-men are now home owners and the number is going up and up.[1] So I don't think she would accept the proposition that we cannot have more and more people owning wealth in this country. She wants to spread wealth ever more widely.

Thus, after the appalling urban riots in Toxteth in Liverpool in July 1981, when the frustrations of hundreds of unemployed, badly-housed no-hopers burst into horrific violence, Mrs Thatcher's reaction was, while startling, all of a piece. Recounted by someone who heard her say it, and not disputed by Lord Whitelaw, it was: 'Oh, those poor shopkeepers.'

Whitelaw:

Yes. I think it might very well have been. I think that this would be her immediate reaction. A lot of people who'd worked very hard to build up a small business of their own suddenly saw it destroyed all at once. She has a great sym-pathy for people who have been building things up for them-selves. Yes, I think probably that is true.

To David Steel, the Liberal leader, this is symptomatic of a larger weakness: her inability to relate to anybody's life or circum-stances which are different from her own, and which include no plan to aspire to be like hers.

Steel:

She would understand, wouldn't she, lower-middle-class people of property having their windows smashed and things taken from the shops. That's what her instinctive reaction would be, to identify with them, whereas of course the prob-lems were very deep seated. And I know, from my own visit to Toxteth, that there was a great resentment at the manner of her appearance in the city, which was to rush in in a police caval-cade, have a quick chat to one or two people and rush out again. She never spends time in the deprived areas of the country, of which Toxteth is only one. It has not been her practice to get down and understand what life is really like for, say, the young black unemployed in Brixton. And I think that's why it feeds

---

[1] The published figures for home ownership are: 1971 49%; 1980 53%; 1982 55%. *General Household Survey 1982*, HMSO, Series GHS No. 12 (1984).

through into her policies and her attitudes, for example, on nationality and immigration, where one is constantly seeing the Conservative party on the one hand proclaiming the virtues of family life and on the other hand destroying family life for many people whose ethos is different from hers.

Gerald Kaufman, Labour's Home Affairs spokesman, agrees that her record on race is questionable:

Kaufman:

One of the interesting things is that despite all the effort the Conservatives make on this matter, the reason why the Asians remain so massively with the Labour party and why the West Indians have not only been massive supporters but massive voters, was because of the statement about swamping that she made in an effort to win that Ilford by-election in March 1978.[1] There's no doubt that it helped the Labour party to win a very difficult by-election in Moss Side in Manchester in July that year. It's never been forgotten and it never will be forgotten. It's gone into the consciousness and embedded itself there. I don't want to say that she's a racialist. To say that somebody is a racialist is in my opinion one of the gravest accusations you can make about anybody. But these were crude, cheap, nasty sentiments that she was trying deliberately to summon up there.

A description he would also apply to her approach to other social questions:

Kaufman:

Her attitude to law and order and crime is narrow, spiteful and vengeful. She really does voice the basest prejudices in the community, and base prejudices exist – they're part of everybody's character, including yours and mine. And she summons up the baser elements in the characters of good people and connects with them.

All of which gives her a weird and ambivalent relationship with the British people.

Kaufman:

People have never seen anything like her. She is a monstrous

---

[1] 'You know, the British character has done so much for democracy, for law, and done so much throughout the world, that if there is a fear that it might be swamped, people are going to react and be rather hostile to those coming in. So, if you want good race relations, you have got to allay people's fears on numbers.' Mrs Thatcher on *World in Action*, Granada Television, 30 January 1978.

phenomenon as far as ordinary people are concerned. This whole strange personality she's manufactured for herself behind a kind of perspex is bewildering to people and they're fascinated by it, of course. It's a class thing really. She's created a kind of class image for herself which is totally alien to ordinary north of England people, I think to a lot of people in the rest of the country too. I don't think that they can link her with their own lives. I remember a few months ago sitting in the West Gorton Working Men's Club and they had a television set as they do in most clubs, up on a shelf in a corner of the room. The ITN 10 o'clock news came on and there she was going around and doing something or other in some place. The conversation stopped and people looked up at her on the screen and I looked not at her but at them. They were looking at her as though she was some strange being; she's totally beyond the experience of ordinary people, in the north of England certainly.

Did Kaufman say class? Surely this cannot be true of the daughter of a mere Grantham grocer? Cecil Parkinson, the son of a railwayman, has risen up the same social scale as Mrs Thatcher. To him the very idea that she could be engaged in class politics is incomprehensible:

Parkinson:

When I hear some of the talk from Mr Scargill for instance, about the class war and so on, and Mrs Thatcher as the warrior in the class war, I think she must find it rather mystifying, because whatever other battle she's fighting she's certainly not fighting the class war.[1] She has no vested interest of any kind in that. When she listens to this talk she must reflect rather wryly about her own background and the way she got to the position she has as a woman with no sponsors but just by her own ability. So I should think she finds this talk about the class war absolutely mystifying.

One can see what Parkinson means. How can someone who's never been one of the toffs conceivably be a throwback to the old era when politics consisted, under the hand of the grandees, of little else but class warfare? However, class politics, as Peter Shore reminds us, need have nothing to do with social origins:

---

[1] For example: 'The strike is no longer about pit closures and pay, it has become a battle for the basic rights of all working-class people against suppression and exploitation by the ruling class.' Arthur Scargill, quoted on BBC news from an interview given to the Russian newspaper, *Trud*, 3 April 1984.

Shore:
Class warfare is back on the agenda of British politics. Class struggle in a sense has always been part of British politics and indeed the parties are still broadly but not too closely aligned to economic and social classes, but the sense that society was moving towards greater classlessness and greater equality has been dominant in the post-war period. Mrs Thatcher's changed that. She's made class struggle much more bitter and rancorous and she has in a very high-profiled way distributed opportunities and income without a blush in favour of those who are already on the top, and has imposed taxes and burdens and reduced benefits for those at the bottom. I don't think any government has done that in any serious way in the whole post-war period.

Peter Shore paints an unattractive picture. So do most of his Labour colleagues. And yet there must be something missing. If Mrs Thatcher is so frightful – so congealed with class hatred, so insensitive to ordinary people's way of life, so divisive and unyielding in her worship of success – how come she's won two elections, with a sporting chance of doing the hat-trick? One reason may be that, among the haves if not the have-nots, she's a populist. To John Gummer, class has nothing to do with it. The common touch goes hand in hand with the almost regal:

Gummer:
She does have a very natural understanding of what the people, the majority, the good hearted, the people who really care about the country, think. I mean, she does have a very natural reaction which is the reaction of the best that's in Britain. She's got a real feel, she isn't out of touch. She's not able to be out of touch because she's by nature in touch. I think that is a quality she has which monarchs in the past have been able to have and which Macmillan had and which I think Disraeli had – a curious way of actually knowing.

She is, in fact, the very reverse of a snob.

Gummer:
She doesn't actually have that superior feeling about ordinary people's views. She does have a real belief that they are worthwhile. She isn't in any way snooty, intellectually snooty, she has a simplicity which enables her to feel for people who say, 'I don't want old ladies mugged on the street. If we hanged the muggers then they wouldn't be mugged on the street.' She manages to disentangle herself from the rather

artificial reactions of the House of Commons, of government, of metropolitan man. She can react as ordinary people do to a series of events, and that's tremendous strength. It's one of the great strengths of leaders in the past in Britain. It's always been true that the best leaders are those who can react as the foot-soldiers would react in any circumstances. She also has a thing about party conferences and about the way in which the constituency parties react. She retains the ability to feel in the way that they feel and yet be intellectually convinced that the answer can't be what they would want it to be. Now that seems to me a very special kind of ability. Most people, having been convinced intellectually, become somewhat arrogant about other people's gut reaction. She's able both to have the gut reaction and to be perfectly convinced of the intellectual conclusion to which she has come.

But this, he claims, doesn't make her a populist:

Gummer:

No, a populist is a much more conscious person. A populist is somebody who knows what is popular and plays to it. She is not that at all. She is a much more subtle person than that. She empathises naturally with what the automatic reactions of ordinary people are on most subjects, and she can hold that empathy even when intellectually she takes a different view.

Yet one of the most consistent opinion-poll findings about Mrs Thatcher belies this. She has always been rated badly for being out of touch with ordinary people.[1] This quite perplexes Lord Whitelaw:

Whitelaw:

I've always found that very surprising. She is immensely in touch with certain feelings. I think it's true that very often she's more in touch with feminine feelings than male feelings on certain social issues. I think that nobody can be in touch with every single section of opinion in the country. She's very much in tune with that section of the community with which she grew up: the shopkeeper world, the country town world. She has a very shrewd opinion as to what the members of our Conservative associations in the country will think. She's very very closely attuned to them and if you decide to go against her

---

[1] Gallup annually ask the question, 'Mrs Thatcher is not in touch with working-class/ordinary people. Do you agree?' In October 1977, 54% agreed. In January 1984, 74% agreed.

you have to reckon you're probably going against a lot of them there. I've always thought that if on any issue she takes a very strong view about what people are thinking as to a very considerable section of the population she will be right, and you are very unwise to go against that feeling without reckoning that a lot of people will share her view.

This is plainly something which even her opponents recognise, though it goes painfully against the grain. Neil Kinnock doesn't sound as if he's entirely sure how to deal with it:

Kinnock:

There is a virility, a political attractiveness about the harshness, but on any test of opinion, when people's values are under examination, they come up with answers and attitudes that are almost diametrically opposed to Mrs Thatcher. So I think that it's the vocabulary of starkness, of firmness, of playground bullies, that appears to be superficially attractive, but doesn't go beneath the surface of the British body politic. So, to the extent that Mrs Thatcher has managed not to lose by this particular form of briskness, I suppose that's to her credit. Whether she's actually accomplished any real change in the political values in Britain is somewhat different. I think that she might be overrated in that respect.

Whether or not she's changed political values, Roy Hattersley certainly doesn't believe that she's changed the intellectual climate:

Hattersley:

There is a strange paradox here. I think Mrs Thatcher is the least intellectual prime minister we have had since the war but by the repetition of a number of slogans which would make a more sensitive politician wince, she has produced a popular reaction – a populist reaction – which has been enormously beneficial to her. She still talks about honest money. I don't think she could define what honest money means, but I think there are a lot of voters who want honest money without having the faintest idea what the cliché entails or what the cliché implies. Similarly she talks about the tyranny of trade union power. I don't believe such a phenomenon exists in this country, but it has struck a chord. Again, one of her virtues as a party leader, though I think one of her disadvantages as Prime Minister, is that she is able to touch these chords, or touch these nerves, or stir people's feelings and prejudices by the simple repetition of a half thought-out cliché which nevertheless is appropriate to some people at this time. I think she has done that in party terms stupendously well.

In most people's terms, this adds up to a pretty good definition of a populist politician. But to Hattersley's former patron and comrade, Roy Jenkins, the prop of popular success rests on a statistical delusion:

Jenkins:

She is a *successful* populist politician. The reason I introduce a note of slight qualification while saying that is that it has to be remembered that she is a successful populist politician mainly because of the British electoral system and the fact that she has been dealing with a split opposition for the first time for fifty or sixty years in this country. Although she has won great parliamentary majorities, she has done so with a small percentage of the popular vote, so there is a contradiction here. I mean it is a most amazing fact that the great populist victory of 1983, producing 397 Conservative seats in the House of Commons, was in fact based on roughly the same percentage of the popular vote as poor Mr Heath's desperate result in 1966, which was the nadir result for the Conservative party at any time since the war.[1]

It's also worth noting that, now, Mrs Thatcher's personal rating in the polls is falling. Only 36% of the population were satisfied with her performance as Prime Minister, according to a Gallup Poll, in May 1985: the lowest figure since before the Falklands War in 1982.[2]

But, populist or not, there's another way she's sold herself and brushed aside potential political damage. She has deployed a lot of cosmetic guile. This could also be termed the Saatchi[3] factor. It must be mentioned, not in order to single her out as a political artist of unusual duplicity, but because her image customarily allows not the smallest trace of cunning to exist within her. Another part of Alderman Roberts' heritage perhaps. Her old Grantham contemporary, Margaret Wickstead, still finds her completely straightforward:

---

[1] In 1966 the Conservatives polled 41.9% of the popular vote; in 1983 they polled 42.4%.

[2] In May 1985 Gallup put Mrs Thatcher's popularity rating at 36%. In July 1982 after the Falklands victory she peaked at 52%. Her lowest rating in office was 25% in December 1981.

[3] Saatchi and Saatchi, the advertising agency which held the Conservative party account for the 1979 and 1983 general elections.

Wickstead:
She's totally honest, I would say. I would never conceive of her doing a dishonest thing. When Mark was trying to get a job, or rather hadn't a job, he was offered – so she told me – several jobs with big firms because he was her son. She said it worried her very much, and I'm sure it did. No, I think she is straight-forward and I think she is honest.

Sir William Pile, a beady-eyed observer of her when she was at the Department of Education, has no reservations on this score either:

Pile:
She was an astonishingly honest politician. She would always represent the facts as she understood them. In the main I never saw her disguise the facts or hide them away. She thought these were part of the public scene and she would stand on them as they were revealed. I remember her once saying when some MP was up on the 1 o'clock news on something or other, 'Why doesn't he tell the truth?'

John Gummer finds this characteristic undiminished by the years:

Gummer:
One thing you do find working with her is that you cannot get away with a half-true statement. I don't mean an untrue statement, I mean just a statement which might be misunder-stood. If you say something she will come back and say, 'What do you really mean by that?' If you suggest she says some-thing, she goes on at it until she feels that what she says is the exact truth. That's why, when we had the Ponting affair earlier in the year, it was so very easy and clear to defend her from the charge that she had not told the truth.[1]

It is no slur upon this paragon, however, to suggest that she has developed some of the skills of the political operator. Would Lord Whitelaw recognise guile as part of her make-up?

Whitelaw:
On major issues she would not fudge. I suppose on some things, smaller things, she would be prepared to. And to that

---

[1] Clive Ponting, a Ministry of Defence official, was acquitted on 11 February 1985 of a charge under Section 2 of the Official Secrets Act of allegedly leaking documents about the Belgrano Affair. The following day in the House of Commons Neil Kinnock said that he did not believe Mrs Thatcher when she denied involvement in the decision to prosecute.
(*Official Report Vol 73 No 59, 12 February 1985*)

extent – perhaps guile is the wrong word. I think she can be extremely flexible on different things. Very much so. And from time to time she uses her feminine charm, and I suppose using your feminine charm is to some extent guile.

She is also far from bull-headed in her personal dealings.

Whitelaw:

She is prepared to consider very carefully how to handle various people in different ways. I don't know whether you'd call that guile. But she is a student of personalities. Not always seen to be so, but is so.

Cecil Parkinson, for a time almost as close as Whitelaw to Mrs Thatcher, shares his perception:

Parkinson:

I think the Prime Minister is a very straightforward person, but she thinks things through very carefully and she anticipates problems and things various people might do, and she's ready to deal with them. And so to that extent she's guileful. She's not just a sort of 'shoot from the hip', totally straightforward, guileless person at all. But I don't mean guileful in any nasty, negative sense. I mean she's a very shrewd person who sees all aspects of the problem before she makes up her mind. I think some people don't believe that, but I certainly do. I don't think, for example, that the media take her by surprise very often. She realises the implications of the things she's doing and saying.

She is also a willing instrument of all the latest wizardry of the political salesman. Before her, after all, nobody had ever heard of Saatchi and Saatchi. Since, she has become famous and they have become immensely rich – partly due to her success in the 1979 election. They are the artificers not of a manufactured politician – if the real Thatcher didn't exist, it would certainly not have been necessary to invent her – but of one whose different and calculated images have long infuriated people like Roy Hattersley and most of her opponents:

Hattersley:

I remember just before the 1979 election talking to Jim Callaghan – I think I give away no secrets by telling you the story – and him saying, 'That woman's going to be packaged; they are going to decide what she ought to be and she is going to be that. I wouldn't do that.' And at the time I wasn't sure that he was right to be so opposed to that sort of artifice. Seeing Mrs Thatcher now, I mean the guile of the voice production, I mean the guile of pretending that she is interested in things that she is palpably not interested in, the guile of associating herself unscrupulously with every popular cause, I've never seen such a politician in terms of unscrupulous association with things that seem likely to win her votes. Guile seems to be her third most prominent characteristic.

Some of Mr Hattersley's colleagues take a rather more scholarly attitude towards her varying guises. Gerald Kaufman itemises her different acts:

Kaufman:

She's got a box-full of personalities. She can pull them out like a change of clothing. We see her in her solemn personality for mournful occasions, with the dark funereal clothes. We see her with her sweetly-smiling act that she's got with children and we also, those of us who sit in the House of Commons, see a very different and a very real Mrs Thatcher. I sit, of course, only a few yards away from her on the opposite front bench. Until very recently, when she was being thwarted or didn't like what people on the other side were saying to her, she would launch into what I can only describe – I hope in an unsexist way – as her 'fishwife' act, screaming away in a shrill, strident voice with her face absolutely contorted. After her recent reverses she has tried to abandon that a bit, no doubt on the advice of her public relations advisers, and we get the sweetly-smiling act most of the time. But I've got to tell you it's beginning to slip again.

This personality, smiling or slipping, has one other shield against the disasters which might otherwise befall such a high-risk politician. To the articulate populist and the practised actress must be added the Prime Minister to whom, on occasion, the government does not even belong. In some ways, it is the most startling of the lot. It's a way of loading the internal debates in her favour, and limiting any damage to herself. As Roy Jenkins describes it, it is oddly un-prime ministerial:

Jenkins:

What I think is her peculiar quality is that she manages at once to be a powerful leader of her government and to detach herself from her government – to be in a sense leader of the government and leader of the opposition at one and the same time. I was very struck, watching her dedicating the memorial in St James's Square to that poor policewoman who was shot in that terrible terrorist incident, when she said, 'These incidents must stop.'[1] Now this was very interesting. It was detaching herself from the government, because if anybody can stop it – I don't think anybody can just by announcing this, but if anybody can – it's the government who can, not the county council or the opposition or whatever. It's the government who can do it, and yet she was saying, 'It's intolerable that this goes on. It ought to be stopped. It ought to be stopped by, not *my* government then, but *the* government. Why doesn't the government stop it?' She does have this curious capacity, which is clever.

Clever for a leader, but sometimes rough on her long-suffering colleagues. Jim Prior is less sanguine. He ran two departments which brought out the most in Mrs Thatcher as leader of the opposition, and from both he still carries the scars.

Prior:

She was undoubtedly a great distancer from policies which she either didn't agree with or wasn't certain they were going to succeed. I mean, that was perfectly true of the industrial relations policy I was pursuing, where the advice being given by Downing Street and Central Office was quite often utterly different from the support and the policy which was coming out of my own department. And when we came to Northern Ireland of course over the Northern Ireland Act of 1982, she made it abundantly clear to anyone who liked to ask her that she just hated the whole thing, didn't want to have anything to do with it and disagreed with everything. And she has a remarkable habit still to this day, of quite often being the leader of the opposition when she wants to be.

A style which makes for acrimony. Where there is discord, may we bring harmony, the saint said. But, although perched on her shoulder as she entered No. 10, St Francis has never made it to the Cabinet.

---

[1] WPC Yvonne Fletcher was shot dead in St James's Square on 19 April 1984 by a gunman inside the Libyan People's Bureau. Mrs Thatcher unveiled a plaque in her memory on 1 February 1985.

The Elder Statesperson of the Western World

First Broadcast: 2 June 1985

No prime minister, on entering office, has had less experience of foreign affairs than Margaret Thatcher. She was born insular, in municipal Grantham, and was fourteen when war broke out. She had insularity thrust upon her by a series of wholly domestic front-bench jobs. How she shook it off – how she achieved, from these unpromising roots, an international dimension – is the subject of this chapter. Once again, as we shall see, the character of the prime minister and her personal obsessions have been critical to what has happened. Upon the orderly, soothing rituals of diplomacy a personality was let loose who scorned them. But what followed was a process of mutual education. As between smooth diplomats and rough prime minister, it's hard to say who has learned the most.

Our first sighting of Mrs Thatcher in the international arena has the merit of rarity. As leader of the Opposition, she set out to learn about the world with typical diligence, and began to make her number with world leaders. At the London summit in 1977 she met President Jimmy Carter. His national security adviser, Zbigniew Brzezinski, remembers a somewhat tentative figure, never seen since:

Brzezinski:

She impressed me then as being very determined, purposeful, not overly well informed on the specifics of international affairs, but certainly having a rather defined world view of her own which she was quite prepared to articulate. I was struck however at the first meeting, in contrast with subsequent meetings, by a certain timidity on her part. She just seemed a little shy or a little uneasy, though that is of course understandable from a human point of view.

Sir Anthony Parsons, later to become her personal foreign policy adviser at No. 10, was between postings at the Foreign Office in London when she became prime minister and was well-placed to observe her first high-level encounters with foreign affairs.

Parsons:

In Cabinet terms, the only post she'd held was Secretary of

State for Education. I think to start with she was very lucky to have an extremely experienced Foreign Secretary for the first few years – a really outstanding Foreign Secretary. And secondly, foreign affairs aren't an exact science, everybody has their own views on most foreign policy problems as indeed she had when she came in. It's much more a matter of feel and having the intellectual ability to grasp the facts of a problem very quickly, which she certainly has. She had a lot of very difficult foreign policy problems thrown at her as soon as she came in, and she was plunged straight in at the deep end, and I think that she did learn very quickly.

Alexander Haig was also impressed by the sharp profile of the Thatcher learning curve:

Haig:

As I recall, my first meeting with her was at the request of some Conservative party friend that I'd known in London during the time when I was Supreme Commander in Europe, and I was asked to speak to Mrs Thatcher during a visit she was making to Brussels after she had become Conservative party leader. It was common for me to do this with aspirants for power from whatever party, and she came to my head-quarters. At that time I noted that she lacked a certain amount of experience and background in security affairs, NATO defence matters, and the related issues which we discussed at some length. On the other hand I also noted that she had a keen interest and insatiable curiosity. That was the first meeting. I met her subsequently I think about a year later, just before she became prime minister, and was astonished to see that she had not only seized control of the brief that we'd had the year before, but was in many respects more knowledgeable than many of the officials with whom I dealt on NATO security affairs.

Characteristically, she was helped in this process by extreme confidence in her own methods. It wasn't long, according to Francis Pym, later to be her Foreign Secretary,[1] before good housekeeping at home began to reach across the far horizon.

Pym:

I think it's fair to say that her experience was very, very limited and I think she tends to look, or did tend to look, and perhaps still does, at international problems as she looks at domestic

---

[1] April 1982–June 1983.

problems and has the approach to them of an extremely practical, down-to-earth housewife who wants to get on with the job. This way isn't always easily understood overseas.
At first bewildering, this approach is now seen to have had some advantages.

Pym:

I think at their first meeting, or the prospect of their first meeting with Mrs Thatcher, quite a number of distinguished people wonder what on earth they are going to confront and what she is going to be like. They find at international meetings that she is as she is at home, extremely direct, doesn't like a lot of talk and waffle, she always comes to the point and when other people wander off she tries to bring them back to the point and they find her very direct and quite formidable to deal with. Some people – some foreigners – find that it becomes irritating after a bit, but nonetheless they respect what it is she is trying to do. And I think they appreciate her irritation that more progress isn't made more quickly. Their style is to take longer about it and to use more words, which is just as foreign to Mrs Thatcher as her approach is to theirs, yet somehow they have got to mix.

The first major overseas meeting she went to was a summit in Tokyo in 1979. It was common knowledge at the time that she was appalled by its sterile rituals and meagre outcome. There was no job to get on with, and she couldn't wait to get back to the serious business of running Britain. All the same, she made a mark. Sir Geoffrey Howe was with her as Chancellor of the Exchequer:

Howe:

There we were amongst these great established figures – Giscard, Schmidt, Carter[1] – and emerging for the final press conference of that occasion, I noticed that the curiosity of the large Japanese audience, including incidentally many Japanese women who were amazed to see a woman assuming primacy in male company, was enormous. She spoke last in the statements they all made to the press conference. She was the only one to do it without notes. She was the only one who achieved a spontaneity and a sparkle that justified the curiosity with which she was first greeted.

---

[1] Valéry Giscard d'Estaing, President of France, 1974–81.
Helmut Schmidt, Chancellor of the Federal Republic of Germany, 1974–82.
Jimmy Carter, President of the USA, 1977–81.

This establishes a point that has remained true: abroad, she has always been box office. It certainly has something to do with her being a woman, and a very striking one. Another trait is personal spontaneity. There is a warmth which those who only see her on a platform might find surprising: Sir Geoffrey, now that he is Foreign Secretary, has seen the effect it can have:

Howe:

I think one of the striking things is the way in which she does establish very good personal relations with a range of people from other countries with whom she has no identity of views or philosophy at all. I think this again is a consequence of her directness. For example, when she met somebody like Mr Gorbachev,[1] the way in which she made it very clear that there was no question of our changing our system to come in line with theirs, and that we didn't look at them through rose-tinted glasses, and didn't expect them to look at us through rose-tinted glasses, is not the way in which all other people would have set the flavour for discussions of that kind.

This directness has become a familiar characteristic. But diplomats have noticed something else about her relationship with the Soviet leader: a reverence for power. Both with Gorbachev and with President Reagan, she exhibits an admiration verging even on coquettishness when face to face with a super-power.

Her very personal responses also infuse discussions with much lesser figures, including Third World Marxists with whom she has nothing whatever in common. Sir Anthony Parsons recalls one such:

Parsons:

She has got great charm. People like her very much. When you are sitting across a table she's enormously informal, she gets down to business very quickly, but in a kind of informal way which people like. I remember when President Machel of Mozambique came, for example, it was tremendous fun – the whole meeting and the lunch afterwards. There was no formality or stiffness about it at all.

Nor is the outcome of these personal encounters always mechanically preordained. Talking to officials after a meeting with President Mitterrand of France, for example, she assured an aide: 'He likes women, you know.' She is also herself susceptible. When

---

[1] Mikhail Gorbachev first met Mrs Thatcher on a visit to Britain, 15–21 December 1984, when he was heir apparent to the ailing President Chernenko.

she was visited by President Ershad of Bangladesh in 1983, she showed it. Britain's aid contribution to Bangladesh had already been fixed, and the Foreign Office brief said not a penny more. The prime minister, naturally, agreed. But she warmed to the President, whose country suffers from affecting human destitution. He walked out of their meeting with twenty million pounds more than he went in with.

The presence of Sir Anthony Parsons at these encounters, however, introduces a harsher question. Why was he there at all? After the Falklands War Mrs Thatcher decided she needed a personal foreign policy adviser, to second-guess the Foreign Office: to mediate, as many saw it, the tension between her gut feelings and the Foreign Office's emollient intellectualising. It was a time when relationships between No. 10 and the Foreign Office were bad, and yet, interestingly, Francis Pym, then Foreign Secretary and widely thought to have increased the rift, doesn't think a mediator should have been necessary:

Pym:
What you might call the international approach, which the Foreign Office and Foreign Secretary would be inclined to take because they negotiate so much, is a kind of attitude that can sit perfectly well with the clean sweep, the fresh approach somebody like Mrs Thatcher takes. I think that approach is something to be harnessed very much to our aid. I wouldn't put it down as a strain. I would say the mix together ought actually to have been more effective than it has been.

Parsons himself was well aware of her antagonism towards the Foreign Office:

Parsons:
I think the prime minister isn't by nature an institutional person. I don't think she's the kind of person who regards the whole bureaucratic institution of government as being *prima facie* a good thing. I think she tends to be naturally suspicious of bureaucracy. I don't think this applies particularly to the Foreign Office, I think it probably applies to the whole Whitehall machine.

Sir Anthony was of course a professional diplomat. He got the job as her personal adviser because he'd had a good Falklands War, as our man at the UN. He was even rumoured to have become, in Thatcherite terminology, 'one of us'. But as a counterforce to the bureaucracy, Parsons of the Foreign Office was not a wholly credible choice. Denis Healey was not the only one to detect in the appointment what he saw as the mandarins' sleight-of-hand:

Healey:

I think the cleverest trick they ever pulled was when she said she wanted an independent source of advice from the Foreign Office. She was persuaded to take Tony Parsons who was a brilliant double agent, who was much more the representative of the Foreign Office to Mrs Thatcher than that of Mrs Thatcher to the Foreign Office.

The evidence shows that the truth is more obscure. The ascendancy has kept changing hands. Certainly the pillars of conventional diplomacy have not crumbled. The Foreign Office has not been captured by chauvinism to the extent that the Treasury was captured by monetarism. But equally, looking no further than Europe, could anyone honestly pretend that it hadn't been a very Thatcherite performance? Abroad as at home, Parsons says Mrs Thatcher has employed her most distinctive attribute:

Parsons:

I think that clarity is essential in the decision-making process, the policy-making process, and this is one of the things I enjoyed when I worked for a year in No. 10. She would go through everything that came over from the Foreign Office, all the documentation, with a microscope and examine every single sentence, and test each sentence for the power of its reasoning, and its clarity of expression, and nothing sloppy or woolly would escape her. Therefore, if all went well, one got total clarity at the point of actually reaching the policy decision.

The earliest exercise in clear-thinking was to persuade not so much others as herself. It concerned the possible settlement of the Rhodesian question, which had dogged British prime ministers for fifteen years. Her liking for clarity, says Parsons, changed her mind:

Parsons:

I think her views on the problem, which I don't suppose she'd studied very deeply, were of a rather right-wing nature when she came in. But what I've always found in working with the prime minister is that she has an extremely good mind, and she is enormously impressed by what one might call cogent facts. Once she'd taken in the facts of the situation, and their implications, she realised there was only one way to proceed.

The baptism of fire was the Commonwealth Heads of Government Conference in August 1979 at Lusaka which set the stage for the Lancaster House Conference a month later.

Parsons:

There's no doubt in my mind that at that Lusaka Conference, which was a very difficult one, semi-public as these affairs are, she did demonstrate that she had already completely mastered the facts of the problem. She showed a remarkable feel, and made a very singular contribution to the fact that the Commonwealth did give us its backing for the Lancaster House exercise, and without that backing, of course, we couldn't have gone ahead.

The key figure here, as Parsons has said, was Lord Carrington, a man vastly experienced in foreign affairs and almost the only member of the Cabinet who, being no kind of threat to her, could make her listen. Denis Healey's image of the pair might even be recognised by Carrington himself, in an irreverent moment:

Healey:

I used to compare him to a zookeeper looking after Rhoda the Rhino who occasionally would break loose and go trotting right through the zoo, and he'd be rushing after her with his cap falling off his head. But she did listen to him. Yes, she did.

Over Zimbabwe, as it became, her personal negotiating tactics, particularly in the Commonwealth, played a crucial role. But the original decision was, as Francis Pym recalls, a rare example of the collective Cabinet view at work:

Pym:

She was persuaded by Peter Carrington to see that the only way of coping with it was the way which, in the end, she did cope with it. The remarkable thing is that when she realised what the score was, and how this would be the best solution for Britain, she took the brief and carried it through brilliantly.

David Steel, the Liberal leader who has long taken a particular interest in the Rhodesian question, wouldn't even give her that much credit. He is dismissive about her personal contribution to the final outcome. How much was it her triumph?

Steel:

I would say not at all except in the negative sense that she withdrew her objections. That's the outer limit of the credit that I would give her. The arrangements were made by Peter Carrington and Christopher Soames[1] and I think they are the

---

[1] Sir Christopher Soames (now Lord Soames) was named as Governor of Rhodesia before agreement was reached at Lancaster House on 15 November 1979. He was in Salisbury from December to Independence Day in April 1980 to supervise the ceasefire and the elections.

people that deserve the credit. Indeed when the previous Labour government was attempting to get a settlement and she was leader of the opposition, the Conservative party was extremely unhelpful, so much so that I took the view from my visits to Zimbabwe – Rhodesia at the time – and the surrounding countries, that there could not be a settlement so long as the Labour government was still there, because anything they tried to do would be undermined by the Conservative opposition. And it would actually take a Conservative government to come to an agreement. Ian Smith[1] and his colleagues in Rhodesia wouldn't do a deal with Labour because they kept on waiting for a change of government. And then, when the Conservative government came into office, I think she was just desperate to be rid of the problem which had thwarted every prime minister, and she gave Carrington and Soames a free hand, withdrew her own stance on the issue and left it to them and they were able to solve it.

If, as Parsons said, she began with a right-wing view on Zimbabwe, this was nothing compared with her views on the Soviet Union. She was and is an extreme and uncompromising anti-Communist. The image of the Iron Lady was just about the alpha and omega of her world view when she came to power. In President Carter's Washington, Zbigniew Brzezinski, himself no mean cold warrior, found this a matter of very special pleasure:

Brzezinski:

When she first came to call on the President, I was struck by the fact that she quoted several times my own works on the Soviet Union. Needless to say, I was very gratified, and more generally I have to say that I found her view on the Soviet Union rather congenial. It seems to me that it involved a great deal of realism.

But was this really very different from the position taken by the Labour governments which preceded her?

Brzezinski:

Maybe not so much in substance as in form and spirit. But in international politics the two are important, both substance and form. It isn't to say that Jim Callaghan was in any way soft on the Soviets. But Mrs Thatcher was clearly more combative, more resolute in her stress on the Soviet danger and the urgent

---

[1] Prime Minister of Rhodesia 1964–79 who declared unilateral declaration of independence.

need for the West to be very tough in its response. And this, of course, was entirely of a piece not only with her lifelong attitude towards Communism, but with that character which is so whole and which, as we've seen time and again, imposes itself almost uniformly on policies across the board. Conservative MP Julian Critchley sees no difference, on this point, between the domestic and the foreign:

Critchley:

She was a fundamentalist. I mean she still is, but in those days to be a fundamentalist was to be remarked upon, was unusual. Margaret is a crusader leaping upon horses the whole time, and if you talk to her about the Soviet Union she would sound like Reagan actually talking about the Commies. She has by sheer force of will elevated the simplicities into the verities, and this was seen at its worst of course in '81–'82 with all the anti-Soviet rhetoric that Reagan, in fact, was also responsible for. Then she suddenly changed her tune, thank God.

After years of megaphone trumpeting, the tone did begin to soften. It may have been little more than gesture politics, but in the international field gesture is often all there is. Why did the gestures change? To each his own interpretation. Sir Geoffrey Howe suggests it came from the stark reality of being in control of the nuclear button:

Howe:

I remember sitting beside her at the party conference two years ago,[1] and listening to the passage in her final speech about the approach we were going to follow towards East–West relations and the passion with which she felt the need to control nuclear weapons. And I saw her adding to her script a spontaneous sentence in which she said 'nobody can realise how strongly I feel this, unless you have been this close as I am to responsibility for these dreadful weapons'. There was a spontaneity and a naturalness about that which commanded respect.

Backbencher Julian Critchley thinks it was all about vote-winning:

Critchley:

I think the simple message got through to Margaret that the more she frightened people into believing that nuclear war was inevitable, the stronger became the peace movement, and somebody made the connection and she understood it.

---

[1] October 1983 at Blackpool.

To the professional diplomat Sir Anthony Parsons, on the other hand, it was an accommodation of the kind the Foreign Office is permanently in business to achieve: a concordat between what they call 'reality' and what a politician parades as an ideological belief – in her case anti-communism:

Parsons:

I don't think for a moment that she's modified that belief in any sense, but I think over the years she's come to work out in her own mind that the Soviet Union and ourselves do inhabit the same part of the planet, we're all part of Europe, that however much we may dislike each other and totally reject each other's *modus operandi*, we have to live together or all of us will die together.

Some people might describe this as a case of a clear Foreign Office victory.

Parsons:

I think that's putting it in too strong terms. Obviously there is a process of dialogue or discussion which goes on the whole time. It's not simply a matter of one single occasion when the Foreign Office advanced on her with a great pile of papers and her coming out of the other end of the meeting saying 'you were right and I was wrong'. This discussion is going on incessantly in different forms: sometimes in set-piece meetings, and sometimes arising out of episodes, sometimes in informal conversations pretty well day to day. But I think as the years have rolled on, her tactical views of the situation have changed.

The Foreign Secretary, Sir Geoffrey Howe, obviously had a hand in this process of dialogue, though he modestly deflects any suggestion that, on getting the job in June 1983, he set about softening the Iron Lady:

Howe:

No, I wouldn't want to suggest that this was Howe saying, 'Gosh, new job, new think, what do we do? This is the answer, must go and sell it to the boss', or anything like that. I think that both of us, having worked together for a long time in foreign affairs as well as in economic affairs, looked at the world scene after the election and thought this is a topic to which we ought to address ourselves. And we did. I did a lot of work on it obviously with advisers, and we discussed it with other colleagues and identified a path along which we ought to begin trying to march. So it wasn't a question of a tussle to persuade Mrs Thatcher to change her view. It was a collectively changed perception, if you like, of the importance of this topic on the international agenda.

It's difficult to know whether this 'collectively changed perception' cut much ice in Moscow. Denis Healey has been an experienced Kremlin watcher for many years, and his visits to the Soviet Union have given him the opportunity to hazard some informed guesses:

Healey:

I think they hated her in her Iron Lady pose, but when the rhetoric changed then they took her more seriously. The fact that Mr Gorbachev chose to come to England before he became leader on his first really extended foreign visit[1] was a tribute to the influence he thinks Britain still exerts over the United States and is prepared to try to exert while Mrs Thatcher is there in her new mood. Now, whether the Russians were so sanguine after Mrs Thatcher's visit to Washington and the extent to which she appeared to give a clean bill of health to the Star Wars concept[2] remains to be seen. But again I think the Russians do not regard personalities as all-important. They look at what they call the objective facts of the situation and they see Britain as having different interests, a different geographical situation, a different history and tradition, a different political environment if you like, from the United States, and therefore are prepared to take Britain seriously. Also I think they are impressed by the extent to which the Foreign Office has tried to build up bilateral links between Britain and the individual countries in Eastern Europe starting with Mrs Thatcher's visit to Hungary.[3]

These differences between the United States and Britain are real enough, and they have not got smaller during the Thatcher administrations. They exist, however, alongside a personal relationship between President and Prime Minister notable for its intimacy. Ronald Reagan was a model for the Conservative Right long before he reached the White House. When he got there,[4] Thatcherism – which has much in common with Reaganism – had been installed across the Atlantic for eighteen months. Ever since he has been Mrs Thatcher's closest international friend and ally.

---

[1] 15–21 December 1984.
[2] 22–23 December 1984.
[3] 2–4 February 1984.
[4] 20 January 1981.

At first sight they are a most improbable couple, he waffling, windy and uninterested in detailed policy: she sharp, direct and a master of every paper that crosses her desk. One feels that if Reagan had been a Conservative MP in her time, the best he could ever have hoped for was a consoling knighthood after twenty years' faithful service in the division lobby. However, they do have similarities. Denis Healey derisively notes one of them:

Healey:
The thing they have in common is that they are both consummate actors. President Reagan was a full-time actor until 1954 and he's an even better actor in the White House than he was in Hollywood. Mrs Thatcher has this extraordinary ability which Reagan has of presenting an image which is attractive to people in the main, the image of resolution, of determination, of not allowing any obstacles to stand in her path. As with President Reagan's image it's very very distant from reality, but very very powerful, and particularly when it isn't competing with an equally powerful image from the other side.

Zbigniew Brzezinski doesn't actually see much difference between the minds of Reagan and Thatcher:

Brzezinski:
I think they are similar in some ways; that is to say they are not particularly complex people. They are – and I do not mean in the least to be invidious – not particularly intellectual in their approach. They are what political leaders ought to be, individuals with a relatively simple but clear grasp of what their priorities are, and they happen to have the willpower to try to implement what they believe in. And those are the essentials of effective leadership, and I think both of them in rather similar ways have that very special quality of leadership.

The President himself thinks any anguish between them, and any disagreements, have been the result of mere misunderstanding:

Reagan:
I don't think any of the disagreements have survived as disagreements once we could talk to each other, some of them might have been the result of distance and not having heard the entire story and when it is told then everything is just fine. But someone asked me once about her as a negotiator. Fortunately we haven't had to negotiate. She would be most formidable on the other side of a negotiating table.

A gracious statement, given the huge imbalance in their relative negotiating strength. Some of the disagreements have gone deep. Along with other European leaders, Mrs Thatcher was deeply irritated by American attempts, as a response to the Soviet invasion of Afghanistan, to stop European companies helping to build the gas pipeline from Siberia to Western Europe. The most glaring example of the imbalance was the American invasion of Grenada in 1983. Should these episodes be seen as evidence of a refreshing British independence from Washington? Labour leader Neil Kinnock is sceptical:

Kinnock:

The Siberian pipeline issue and the Grenada issue could have given the opportunities for independence of action and I think that's a function of a good friend, to tell another good friend when they're wrong. But how has it turned out? In terms of the Siberian pipeline, I think it was the German arguments that really held the day rather than Mrs Thatcher's, and I wouldn't want to subtract from any credit that she could get there because I think the German line was the right line. In terms of Grenada, well the consequences are nil. We are not exerting the influence that we should in the Caribbean countries, and we could exert in the Caribbean countries because of our cultural, trading and historical links. Unfortunately, in the wake of Grenada, no progress has been made in that direction.

Alexander Haig thinks Mrs Thatcher was right to be severely put out about Grenada. He was no longer Secretary of State then – but Haigspeak lives on.

Haig:

I think we failed to consult appropriately. After all, Grenada was a member of the Commonwealth. The prime minister was facing a meeting in which she could have walked into an extremely hostile and counter-productive venue. She was surprised late at night by being put on notice, and I am quite confident that she has enough spirit in her marrow to have reacted less than favourably, influencing what otherwise might have been a more favourable demeanour on her part.

But to Reagan himself it was just one of those unfortunate, if inescapable, breakdowns in communication:

Reagan:

It was unfortunate at the time. My situation was not one of lack of trust in her or on your side of the ocean, but in this city of ours, Washington, the walls seem to have ears. I felt it was so important in the limited time that we had to plan and move after the decision actually to send the troops on their way – I was so fearful of a leak from our side – that I put it on close-hold, because there were so many lives involved. And the minute we could I explained to her what our situation had been and why I had made the decision I made.

No words can really dress up what an embarrassment this was in London. Nor is there much disguising the fact that, on large questions, the traffic of influence goes one way only. On Star Wars, the futuristic American dream of strategic defence in space, Mrs Thatcher's serious doubts were codified into a four-pronged statement of acquiescence.[1] Britain would go along with it so long as it was not aimed at nuclear superiority and did not undermine deterrence, was accompanied by continuing arms-reduction talks, and would not be carried beyond the research stage without negotiations. Likewise on the dollar and interest rates, Reagan's private assurances have, in practice, meant insultingly little. She was publicly humiliated by him when in February 1985, after she had addressed an ecstatic Congress on the need for America to reduce interest rates and curb the dollar, the President told the press before she was even on her plane back to London that the recovery of America's trading partners was up to them. As this incident shows, like every other British prime minister, she has to accept the brute realities of power. Thus Anthony Parsons thinks private influence is the most she can hope for:

Parsons:

I think the prime minister believes very strongly that the United States is absolutely vital to us, and that obviously one of the cardinal planks of our policy must be the best possible relations with the United States. By the same token, I think she believes that we can only hope to influence the United States in private and affect their judgements over various issues where we may disagree, if the basic relationship is extremely good. I think she has demonstrated with the Reagan administration a feel for how to achieve all these objectives.

Neil Kinnock, predictably, interprets the relationship somewhat differently:

Kinnock:

I think to say she was his lapdog would be possibly overstating it. I do think that the special relationship is now less healthy

---

[1] In Washington, on 23 December 1984.

than it should be. We will not be technologically or commercially or militarily the equals of the United States of America, but this is Britain and without any overdeveloped sense of pomposity or self-importance I think we've got a great deal more to give to the world than following just about every twist and turn of a rather twisted and turning American foreign strategy, which even friends of the administration frequently counsel against.

Etienne Davignon, Belgian member of the European Commission from 1977–84, takes a rather more pragmatic view of the situation:

Davignon:
My interpretation would be that the President of the United States, at certain moments in the history of the United States, whoever he might be, is jolly well going to do what he wants to do, whoever is speaking to him. And I would imagine that this was not lost on Margaret Thatcher. There are limits to the influence you can have on the President of the United States and I think it's an experience a number of British prime ministers have gone through. This does not affect the closeness of the relationship but at any given moment the President of the United States is going to follow his policy, if he's sure that is the best one, especially if he feels it's working. Certainly that's the case with Reagan now. He would like to be nice, but not at the expense of changing his policy.

But former West German Chancellor Helmut Schmidt finds it disappointing that the only European leader who could claim a naturally warm relationship with the President has not managed to exploit it:

Schmidt:
I think, given the personal chemistry between Ronald Reagan and Margaret Thatcher, that vis à vis America, she would be a very good spokesman for the interests of the Europeans in some of those fields which matter most in international politics right now, which are firstly international economics, and secondly western grand strategy vis à vis the Soviet Union. I think she would be a perfect communicator to Ronald Reagan, but this would presuppose that the Europeans had a common analysis of their interests in these fields which obviously they lack right now.

Denis Healey identifies two major areas where her failure to influence Reagan has let Europe down:

Healey:
One is the Middle East where the Venice Declaration,[1] which Britain helped to mastermind and which she very solemnly endorsed at the time, has really come to nothing because Britain has not been prepared to argue with the Americans over it. The other, which could turn out to be a great deal more important, is Central America where the Europeans are deeply worried that America may stumble into a war which would undermine popular support for the alliance and perhaps distract the United States' attention from the rest of the world to South America for a generation. Britain has tended to side with Reagan over that rather than with the Europeans, who have shown a great deal more courage, not only President Mitterrand but also Chancellor Kohl and the West German Foreign Secretary, Herr Genscher.

The absence of the common analysis Schmidt referred to obviously has many causes, rooted in different national interests. But it has to be said that one of the larger causes is that Mrs Thatcher – now, by dint of long service, the elder statesperson of the western world – does not see Europe in terms of a grand vision. Roy Jenkins does. He was President of the European Commission from 1977–81 and is scornful of her approach:

Jenkins:
I don't think she has any feeling for Europe as an idea, but equally, I think she is totally committed to keeping Britain in Europe which I very much welcome. I think she would regard it as very bad that we should come out. But she has no idea of contributing anything positive to the relaunch of Europe, which Europe desperately needs at the present time.

For her it has become a counting house, above all the place where we get 'our money' back – to which end she has relentlessly harangued her so-called partners for most of six years. This, for Roy Jenkins, poses another question:

Jenkins:
Is she a good negotiator? Has she got a better deal for Britain than other prime ministers would have got in the circumstances? I generally find this rather a difficult question to answer. I think as a negotiator – no, not as negotiator, that's not quite the word – as a proponent of the British case, she

---

[1] Made at the Council of Ministers meeting on 12/13 June 1980 in Venice. It stated that the Palestinians must be 'associated' with any peace plan.

does have the advantage of being almost totally impervious to how much she offends other people. She has this virtue, this conviction of self-righteousness. And therefore I have seen her when she was a new prime minister surrounded by others who were against her and being unmoved by this in a way that many other people would find difficult to withstand. But I would make a strong criticism of her negotiating technique. To be a good negotiator you probably have to do two things; you have to take a strong position, and open up something, and then you have to know when it's right to settle. I think she's good at taking a strong position and making other people slightly frightened at what'll happen if they don't get a settlement, but she has no idea when to settle.

Maybe there was no other way she could have done it – but her method had a cost.

Davignon:

Discussions at the European level at those types of meetings are directly influenced by the personalities. And that is what counts at the end because it is people discussing with other people on issues. It's not the normal procedural activity of decision-making where briefs count. I think what could have been dangerous, and I think at some moments was dangerous, was the surprise of her partners and the resentment that some of her partners bore at being roughed up, which made them more negative than they would otherwise have been.

There's not much doubt that this roughness did secure Britain some advantages. But not perhaps as many as Mrs Thatcher was looking for in all those years of struggle. When it was put to Sir Geoffrey Howe that the final deal on the Community budget at Fontainebleau in June 1984 was in fact one which, for a long time, she had not wanted to accept, he did not demur:

Howe:

Yes, but the basis on which we concluded it was remarkably close to the original objectives we set ourselves four, five, six years before – I can't remember, we were at it for so long, '79 to '84 – five years before. As with all these things you came to a moment of decision, of making the last move and the last counter move, and there was no doubt in her mind, no doubt in our mind, that that was the moment to make that choice.

The question, however, has a larger dimension. What has the Thatcher government, with its long life and its impregnable majority, done for Europe, as opposed to its own short-term interests? What even has it done, in the eye of history, for Britain's longer-term position? Francis Pym was for a year her Foreign Secretary. He is pessimistic:

Pym:

I think the way the budget negotiations were conducted over so long a time has done Britain a certain amount of harm in Europe. I think the leaders of European countries have felt that we haven't been altogether reasonable and sensible. Of course the popular view in this country is that you bang the table and say 'we must have our money', but actually we do need the European Community, the whole of Europe needs the European Community. It is stuck in a rut at the moment and it needs a great deal of political leadership to get it moving. I don't myself think that this particular aspect has been terribly well done.

Roy Jenkins goes further. He thinks the last five years have been one long, missed opportunity:

Jenkins:

I would have said that what was most in Britain's interest was to achieve a leadership role comparable with that of France and Germany. And I think by negotiating roughly – by grocer's economics if you like – she has completely thrown away the opportunity for Britain to achieve, not a single leadership position, but a position of one of the tripod of leadership which has constantly eluded us for years past. And I think that has been a loss of opportunity, far greater than any hundreds of millions which she's gained by saying 'I want my money back'.

On the other side of the Channel, how would Etienne Davignon describe feelings about her?

Davignon:

I would say at this moment there is a dual feeling. There is genuine feeling of respect for somebody who stands up to the majority. In most European countries she would certainly be considered as a great personality. I think the 'Dame du Fer' presentation is exaggerated, and not how people really see her, but they perceive a tough personality, yes. Tough in the negative sense, because that personality is used more for the benefit of the United Kingdom than for the general good, and here it is felt that the balance is too much for the United Kingdom and not enough for the group. Everyone accepts that you will not be a good leader if you don't take care of the interests of your country, but we feel here, certainly in smaller countries, that to do that you must also get the group to perform. And if you get the balance wrong then it won't work. The feeling is that she's got the balance wrong.

Helmut Schmidt, bleakly brooding in retirement from the stage he once dominated, shares this European perception and feels a bitter personal disappointment:

Schmidt:

I must confess that by and large my expectations have not come true: Britain has not taken the political lead within the EEC in any of the problematic fields. By and large the Community is still waiting for British experience and pragmatism to become devoted to the common causes of Europe.

He is also sceptical of the claim that recent negotiations over the budget constitute any kind of success for Margaret Thatcher:

Schmidt:

There is no success and I will add just as a footnote that I warn anybody in Europe – whether he is Italian or Irish or Spanish or Greek or German or British – against calling it a success if he prevails in any question, by a slight edge in the hand of the negotiations, in maintaining what he thinks is the national interest of his country. The most ridiculous thing, for instance, is that for the last couple of years these European summits have concentrated on agricultural policy and its financing. You have about 5% of the European population in farming but you have more than twice the number – namely 11% of Europeans – who are without a job. So it is rather to be expected that they would devote at least twice as much time to the question of how jointly to overcome this mass unemployment than how jointly to add to the well-being of farmers. But they would all rather talk about farmers and how to finance the subsidies of farming products, than about general economics. So I would be rather careful not to talk about success in the European Community. We have had this mass unemployment since 1980/81 which was the consequence of the structural shock to the economic fabric of the world's economy after the second oil price explosion and all that went with it, and as a consequence of that, we now have the debt problem in South America and so on. There has been no success by the European Community in dealing with these questions – no success whatsoever – neither Margaret's nor François Mitterrand's nor Kohl's nor anybody's.

These are deep waters. The measure of success in something so complex as the geopolitics of the world economy is not easily defined. Nor can one quantify the benefits of such a narrowly 'patriotic' policy as Mrs Thatcher seems to pursue. That she is patriotic few would deny, but the idea that she is somehow more patriotic than anyone else makes other politicians bristle. Geoffrey Howe's response to such a suggestion was terse:

Howe:

Everybody is patriotic.

Neil Kinnock's was more elaborate:

Kinnock:

Mrs Thatcher does exploit the flag. I think that is something which the British people will take only so far. When they think that the use of words about destiny or patriotism are replacements for real policy or tangible accomplishments, they become extremely suspicious. When for instance you match up the abolition of exchange controls with Mrs Thatcher's form of patriotism, and it's measured in terms of thousands of millions of pounds of desperately needed investment capital leaving the country every year, the patriotic drum sounds a little bit hollow. The novelty of Mrs Thatcher, her use of language, her particular approach to politics, certainly gained her ground in her first six or seven years as leader of the Conservative party, during much of which time of course she was prime minister. When it is repeated continuously it becomes like an old song, and instead of people tapping their feet they begin to scratch their heads and wonder why there isn't a new song.

The one act of foreign policy where naked patriotism brought Mrs Thatcher tangible political benefits was the decision to go to war over the Falkland Islands. The victory over the Argentines sent Mrs Thatcher's popularity-rating shooting up. At one level the Falklands War was a shattering irrelevance in British foreign policy: at another it's an episode etched as deeply into Margaret Thatcher's psyche as it must be into any truthful account of her political survival. It was the determining event, many would say, of the 1983 election – and one where President Reagan marked her performance as perfect:

Reagan:

I don't know how it could have been improved. I think she was faced with a very grim necessity, and I think it was well handled. But I think it also was the result of her ability at decision making and firm action.

His Secretary of State at the time was Alexander Haig. Haig doesn't think her main motive, during those crucial weeks when he was attempting to negotiate a peace settlement, was as narrowly nationalistic as it appeared:

Haig:

No, although like all good internationalists, she has a deep and abiding smattering of self interest – and national interest – in everything she does, she is indeed an internationalist. Throughout the Falklands crisis it was very evident that she was more concerned, perhaps even more than with the issue of the vital interest of Britain and of its standing around the world, that this should not be a major setback once again of a western democracy in the eyes of the totalitarian east and the Soviet Union, which could have ramifications and subsequent miscalculations that could risk peace in the world.

It was at this moment she lost her most trusted foreign affairs adviser. Lord Carrington resigned and Francis Pym was appointed in his place:

Haig:

He had just arrived in office. And it was clear that his position was not on the prime minister's wavelength at that moment.

Pym was thought to be the dove, and she the hawk. But, negotiating with her, Haig found her less rigid than was popularly supposed:

Haig:

There were a number of pressures from Conservative backbenchers to take a very rigid line, not only on the question of self-determination, but on the question of sovereignty, and I found the prime minister more than willing to meet reasonable propositions half-way, and even beyond half-way as she did in the last American-devised – I'll call it Haig-devised – proposal that I brought to her. She didn't accept it – it wouldn't be fair for me to say she would have ultimately – but she certainly authorised me to go forward and present it.[1]

The Falklands War was many different things to different people. For Mrs Thatcher, it is emblematic of two features of her approach to foreign affairs: first, her inexperience, which is where we came in, and second, the resources of character with which she made up for this. Unlike some of the War Cabinet, she had never seen battle. She had to take lessons from Lord Whitelaw:[2]

---

[1] For details of the negotiation see Max Hastings and Simon Jenkins, *The Battle for the Falklands*, Chapter 6.
[2] Lord Whitelaw was an officer in the Scots Guards from 1939–47.

Whitelaw:

I was always very clear on one simple point: that those at the top must be prepared to accept casualties and must never give the feeling to those who are commanders in the field that you aren't prepared to accept casualties. And I took it upon myself to say to her how important it was, to steel oneself when there were casualties. And she was marvellous. I think that was a point where perhaps one was able to help from one's knowledge of war.

War, according to Sir Frank Cooper, then the Permanent Secretary at the Ministry of Defence, brought out precisely the qualities most natural to her: guts, clarity and that piercing certainty about what to do:

Cooper:

Because she'd never been personally involved in actual fighting or in a war, there were some things, you know, which you didn't see with the same clarity, or obscurity, or probably both, in anything like the same degree as someone who'd actually been in a war. I've come actually to a very curious view on this, namely, that I think it was probably an advantage that she hadn't been in that kind of situation. If she had, she might have been more plagued by self-doubt and questioning than in fact she was.

Lord Lewin, then Admiral Lewin, Chief of the Defence Staff, endorses this view:

Lewin:

Of course she was too young even to be involved, except as a schoolgirl in the last war, and to that extent was bound to rely rather more heavily on military advice that perhaps somebody who had served in the last war, or had done National Service. Mind you, I think that the sort of experience of that sort of person would not have been related to high-level crisis management and they might have been misled into thinking they knew all about it, when in fact they didn't.

They might though, as Lord Whitelaw explained, have had experience of casualties. She hadn't, and wasn't prepared for it:

Lewin:

We were fortunate to have a fairly gentle lead in to casualties. It happened just before our repossession of South Georgia when we were trying to put in special service forces to do reconnaisance and the weather was appallingly bad, and we lost two helicopters in a terrible snowstorm. It was the first military event of the Falklands War and we thought we'd lost 22 men to begin with. John Nott and I had to go across to No. 10 and break the news to the Prime Minister that this was how this particular operation had started and it was a shock. Fortunately within half an hour we'd got the news that in fact nobody was lost – the helicopters were lost but nobody was injured and everybody was safe.[1] And so that was a gentle introduction. Of course, later on, we did lose a helicopter full of SAS men, 22 men in one go, before we'd begun the landing.[2] But I think she had time to think about it by then, so when it did happen she had prepared herself for it. Her reaction then was very very robust, sad of course, we were all sad, but because of this introduction which had turned out happily I think she had thought about it a bit and come to terms with it. I explained to her that this was going to happen and this was the sort of experience we had in the last war. I can remember the nights on the convoys when six merchant ships sailed and they were not there in the morning, night after night.

This lack of previous military experience didn't, he observed, make her cautious.

Lewin:

I think cautious is the wrong word – determined, prepared to weigh up the risks and make a judgement and make a decision and stick by it. She was a decisive leader which is what of course the military want. We don't want somebody who vacillates, we want to be able to put the case to her, the requirements to her, and say this is how it is, this is the decision we want, we want it now and we want it quickly and we don't want a wishy-washy decision, we want a clear-cut decision. She was magnificent in her support of the military.

This military milieu and these military requirements, once she'd got on top of them, conformed closely with Mrs Thatcher's instincts and character. She has rarely been accused of failing to make a decision – rather more often of making the wrong one. In the Falklands, it all came out right, assisted by her lack of self-doubt. Such emphatic self-assurance can also, of course, be a great advantage in the subtler world of diplomacy, particularly when you're selling Britain, which Mrs Thatcher often seems happiest doing. But what vision does she have of the wider world where the challenge is rather more diffuse than the business of

---

[1] 21 April 1982.
[2] 20 May 1982.

reclaiming 'our money', or recapturing 'our territory'? Having got over their first surprise, and often admiration, will the world's leaders have any continuing reason to learn from the leader who's been there longer than any of them? With the Thatcher era destined to last for some years more, the question for the future is perhaps whether she can prove that Neil Kinnock's hearsay evidence is mistaken.

Kinnock:

I don't think she's got an international vision. I think that she's got an idea of her own position. I speak as you would expect from time to time to people who meet her on an equal footing as leaders of their countries, and I'm not betraying confidences when I say that initially they are very impressed by a woman, and that isn't the least bit sexist because it's to her credit that she is the first woman party leader and the first woman prime minister in Britain, nobody can take that away from her. They are very impressed by that. They are impressed by her assertiveness, and it's only on the second and third and fourth time of meeting that they realise that the same music is being played, the same style, the same content, and no effort at organisation, no deftness of operation – she's not fleet of foot in argument and debate – will disguise that. So the initial, very favourable impression, gathered by people who don't share her politics, evaporates over a period of time.

Mr Kinnock says that, of course, from the very standpoint she started with: complete inexperience in foreign affairs. But Mrs Thatcher has come a long way since that first timid tiptoe into Jimmy Carter's antechamber. She has learned a lot. She has lived by the rules of diplomacy as much as they have been changed by her. She knows how to play the modest hand she holds. Such terms as 'global vision' and 'the world order', however, she probably mistrusts as deeply as when she was the newest leader, and was first introduced to them by her fellow-summiteers in a Japanese tea-garden six long years ago.

The Glorious Revolution?

First Broadcast: 9 June 1985

Margaret Thatcher proposes herself as an historic phenomenon. She has surveyed the past and found it wanting. She has scanned the future and been seized by a sense of destiny. She has a mission, she believes, to wipe out past delusions and set Britain on a future course towards recovery, prosperity and an absence of socialism. This is a very personal mission. She is no ordinary political leader, content to peg along keeping the show on the road. She has made great claims, fixed high ambitions, and invited the country to suffer in order to attain them. By that standard she must now be judged. Has it been – can we expect it soon to become – a truly glorious revolution?

This can only be an interim verdict. But elections are interim verdicts too. Voters are their own historians. We can begin to map out the ground for judgement, understanding with Roy Jenkins, a professional historian, how hazardous it would be to make too many assumptions.

Jenkins:

What is certainly the case is that she will have been prime minister for a long time, too long I think. She may exceed Asquith and be the prime minister for the longest period this century, the longest period since Lord Liverpool.[1] Well, Asquith's reputation – I don't wholly agree with this – is not very high at the moment. And Lord Liverpool's has always been non-existent. So, being prime minister for a long time is not in itself a guarantee of great achievement and most of the people on both sides of the Atlantic who are looked back on now as being major figures did not have a very high repute at the time they were in office. Certainly Truman did not in America. Certainly Attlee did not here. Lincoln, curiously enough, did not in America – Lincoln's reputation was remarkably low during the whole period of the American Civil War. And I think it's very difficult to judge what history will say about people. The other things Truman, Attlee and Lincoln had in common, of

---

[1] Herbert Asquith, Prime Minister and leader of the Liberal party 1908–1916; Lord Liverpool, Prime Minister and leader of the Tory party 1812–1827.

course, was the relative brevity of their time in office. The same ominous message, that length of service does not necessarily guarantee permanence of impact, comes from the other side of the world and the other end of the political spectrum. Political leaders of every hue have in common a desire to leave some enduring mark. But the Labour leftist Michael Meacher brings unhappy tidings from the east:

Meacher:

I went to China in 1972, four years before Mao Tse-tung died, and I was certainly told that this man, the most remarkable man in the 20th century, had transformed the mentality and the attitudes and the consciousness of one billion Chinese people, and it seemed very credible at the time. He died in 1976 and it is now perfectly clear a decade later that the inheritance of Mao Tse-tungism, Red Bookism and all of that has been totally transformed. Maybe there are vestiges left but it is nothing like the way it looked fifteen years ago. I still suspect that when Mrs Thatcher finally goes, much less that she has created and generated will remain than we would think now.

That's a question we'll be looking at in this final chapter. What nobody could doubt is that she still holds strong to the idea that fundamental change is possible and that she is the person to lead it. The problems come round year after year, many of them in truth not soluble. But there's no trace here of the weariness or pessimism which has soon afflicted most of her modern predecessors. Perhaps she made John Gummer chairman of the Conservative party in 1983[1] because he echoes her bright-eyed enthusiasm:

Gummer:

I think the really remarkable thing about her as a person is that she's been leader of the Tory party for ten years and it still fascinates her. Even when you're discussing something which she must have discussed a dozen times before or you're going through the same point in the public expenditure round or discussing the same position about some foreign affairs issue which she must have been through ten or eleven times, she's still fascinated by it, keen to get it right, keen to learn from what she got partly wrong before, very interested in the way in which it'll pan out. You never go in and find that she is feeling it's not worth talking about that subject today. Now that, I think, is unique.

---

[1] He was replaced in September 1985 by Norman Tebbit.

Even at the tenth time of asking, moreover, these discussions can still generate that freshly heated exuberance which some ministers find damnably unsettling. One such delicate spirit – to whose type Mrs Thatcher's style has still made no mellowing concessions – was the former Transport Secretary David Howell:

Howell:

I find raising the temperature when one's discussing difficult issues and turning the discussions into arguments a very time-wasting business. In that situation people give confused replies which are quick rather than carefully thought replies which may not be so quick. And I'm not sure that things always turn out for the best if you keep the temperature at boiling point. In fact, you could argue that over public expenditure and taxation, where we have not made the progress over the years we should have done, these were precisely issues where constant high-temperature battling has been less effective than a more calm and measured approach might have been.

With this goes the one human weakness which her most devoted admirer, Keith Joseph, will admit to noticing:

Joseph:

I tell you something she's not good at; she's not very good at relaxing, taking time off, that's the nature of the creature, God bless her, I think.

Ian Gow, her parliamentary private secretary in her first term and constantly at her side, denies that she's Superwoman:

Gow:

I think there's a misunderstanding – people say that the prime minister doesn't need sleep. The truth of the matter is that there is a perpetual triumph of the spirit over the flesh and she drives herself extremely hard. She has made herself do without sleep, but of course she gets extremely tired.

And, given the schedule she sets herself, that's hardly surprising.

Gow:

She used to get up every day at half past six. Whereas other people might say to themselves 'I won't finish that box tonight', she used to always finish her boxes the night before, and it was two and three o'clock in the morning before they were done. That was normal. When we were doing a speech it was five or six o'clock in the morning, and then she would have perhaps an hour's sleep and get up and look much fresher and more sprightly than any of us. We used to arrive back in the morning feeling rather weary and there she was looking just as alert and vigorous and ready for the day as if she'd had eight hours of sleep.

This lifestyle leaves room for few diversions: few books, no recreations, no frivolities, no corners to which the soul retreats, which have nothing whatever to do with the extraordinarily demanding business of running the country. But John Gummer says this is because politics itself is an occupation of almost limitless scope:

Gummer:

I don't think she is an unrelaxed person in the sense that she's taut or tightened up all the time – very often in the kind of discussions you have with her she is relaxed. But she enjoys politics. That is her relaxation. And politics is such a multi-faceted thing that she relaxes by a change of pace and change of subjects. I mean she doesn't relax in the sense she collects stamps – it's not that kind of relaxation. I don't think she finds it easy to relax and she'd admit that she doesn't find it easy because she finds it all absorbing – but only because she plays it right across a very wide field. And some prime ministers have actually only been personally involved in those bits of politics they're interested in. Now, although she's dominated by the belief that we have to get the economics right, she is fascinated by so many other things in politics that she can relax into some other subject.

This shows a measure of earnestness not entirely to the taste of public admirers like the veteran Tory MP Sir Edward du Cann:

Du Cann:

Where some of us would curl up with a good book she likes to curl up with a posse of people and have a great discussion about policy with them.

John Hoskyns, for three years the head of her policy unit in No. 10, was present at a few such occasions:

Hoskyns:

I can certainly remember having after-dinner whisky in the flat with David Wolfson and Alan Walters,[1] generally chewing the cud about where we had got to and how things were going. Yes, she was quite ready to do that, I always felt it would have been good for her psychologically to do more of that but she

---

[1] Sir David Wolfson, chief of the political staff at No. 10 1979–; Sir Alan Walters, the Prime Minister's personal economic adviser 1981–3.

always drives herself so hard. I think that type of thing – sitting back, relaxing, being able to talk freely when you know you are not facing adversaries in the House, having arguments across the table, talking with people you know are basically trying to help you – is terribly important for anybody in a top job because top jobs get lonely. She did more of that than people realise, but I would have liked to have seen more of it.

But even on these occasions she showed no taste for politicians' tittle-tattle, Here, as elsewhere, she sets her sights high. To the very reverent Ian Gow, they are fixed on nothing less than the ceaseless pursuit of an almost sacred duty:

Gow:

I think that her main interest in her friends is discussing with them how best we can restore some of the qualities which she admires and others admire, which used to be the characteristics of the British people. That includes a deep patriotism and pride in the country and it also includes a commitment to rewarding success, free enterprise, a non state-dominated Britain.

However, this is just the problem. These are large ambitions, bespeaking a great vision and a grand strategy. What evidence is there that such commodities are in adequate supply? Clearly, the larger and more risky the objective, the more crucial is the long-term plan for meeting it. If you're not careful, day-to-day detail keeps getting in the way, especially if you're as interested in it as Mrs Thatcher. All her colleagues bear the scars of this prime-ministerial appetite – Norman Tebbit, for instance:

Tebbit:

I guess there are not very many ministers in government that haven't had the rather embarrassing experience of finding out that she knows more about one aspect or another of one's department than one knows oneself. Very difficult, that sort of thing. It's marked by the way she takes on Prime Minister's Questions. She expects herself to have a command of everything that's going on in the government and she has the energy to absorb those facts.

John Gummer, too:

Gummer:

No minister in the government could possibly be unaware that she might well know about some very minor decision that he made because she has a very very great capacity for absorption of information. She's very disconcerting sometimes because she will remember something that you've said to her months ago and she'll remember it absolutely, and it'll come out. It's very often from a conversation when you weren't quite sure whether she was actually listening because something else was going on at the time, but she'll come up and say, 'Well, you did say that to me. Now how does that square with what you're saying now?' That's an impression that gets right round Whitehall. And what a contrast with Callaghan. One of the interesting things is the direct contrast between them in sheer volume of work she gets through. Callaghan, one felt, had no real influence outside the immediate circle whereas she is felt throughout Whitehall in a very real way because she is very practically involved in all it does.

A telling little episode, illustrating just this point, is recalled from the days when her popularity was at its lowest by David Howell:

Howell:

We were very concerned in the autumn of 1981 with the strategic direction of the government and how on earth we were going to be in shape to win the next election. And I think a number of people – and I was certainly one of them – did put to the Prime Minister the need for some clearer strategic thinking. But I do have to say that, on the whole, the Prime Minister was inclined to say to those sort of representations, 'Don't bother me with strategy, I have to be up all night rewriting press releases and getting speeches straight as it is.'

Reg Prentice, rewarded for leaving the Labour party by being given office in the first Thatcher government, felt that the obsession with detail virtually excluded any systematic thought about the future at all:

Prentice:

I think she tends to interfere too much in the decisions that properly belong to her Cabinet ministers and to other people in the hierarchy. That is not good for them, and doesn't make for good government. And she doesn't give herself enough time to think the policies forward. This is what I think is missing in the government at the moment, has been for some time, a lack of a forward strategy. The election manifesto in 1983 was good in parts but very bad in other parts – the references to local government for example – partly because of Margaret Thatcher's disinclination to have a forward-policy unit within the government or within the Conservative party, or indeed to devote time herself to these long-term problems.

Now some of this has become, these days, a condition of employment as a national leader. Everywhere you look the job has changed. It's not simply the workaholic obsessions of a woman who declines to delegate which prevents her from developing a long-term strategic vision. Viscount Davignon, the worldly Belgian Eurocrat, sees the demands of day-to-day detail burying almost every aspiring statesman's approach to big questions:

Davignon:
There is much less time for these types of questions because the difficulty of the routine task of being prime minister, the day-to-day business, has become so great. Having less time for long-term thinking, you have less interest in it. So discussing it becomes a formality. You will go and see somebody, but if you can do it in six hours you will do it in six hours. Before you'd have done it in three days and had more time to think and talk. I think that's one of the changes – it's the consequence of being so tied up with trying to settle immediate things which you just can't push away, and of the task of explanation of policy which is much greater in 1985 than it was before. Before, you explained here or there; now if you can't explain everything you do, you are going to be in difficulty. I think on the whole that's a good thing, but it takes a great amount of time. And of course it is at the expense of having time to think and find occasions to look at the big questions. I think this is one of the illnesses of Europe at this stage. Mid-term is the end of the week and long-term might be the end of the year.

All the same, our own leader's particular propensities are probably only too well attuned to these pressures. The aftermath of the carnage at the European Soccer Cup Final in Brussels in June 1985[1] showed her at her most typical. Instantly engaged: instinctively tuned into public attitudes: patriotically shattered by the damage done to Britain's reputation: demanding action this day. But also more interested in the executive detail than in the elusive search for constructive social philosophising. Sir Anthony Parsons saw this trait when he worked at No. 10 as her foreign policy adviser:

---

[1] On 29 May 1985 thirty-nine people died when Liverpool fans attacked supporters of the Italian club, Juventus, on the terraces of the Heysel Stadium, Brussels. On 30 and 31 May Mrs Thatcher held emergency talks with ministers and football officials and pledged to tackle soccer hooliganism. The subsequent 'Sporting Events (Control of Alcohol) Bill' was rushed through the House of Commons, unopposed, on 3 July 1985.

Parsons:

I think she has got a vision, but I think her kind of intellectual character is one which does tend to concentrate very much on the problem of the day, the problem at hand. Equally, I think she has got what I must say I find very endearing, she has a distrust of grandiose phraseology and broad-brush rhetoric. I don't think this means that she hasn't got a broader vision, but rather that she actually prefers as a person to get on with the job, rather than to pontificate in a lordly way about global matters.

Francis Pym appears to find it less endearing:

Pym:

I don't think she's somebody who likes to sit and ruminate for an hour or two alone for a whole day about the country and what might be done. She likes to get on with something that is practical and realistic, and I think she regards anything that is contemplative or thoughtful as a waste of time. She particularly enjoys criticism – she's a brilliant critic of other people, she really relishes castigating others, but I don't hear her make creative speeches, thoughtful, forward-looking speeches. I don't think she has the capacity to lift the nation's eyes to the future, that isn't part of her. And therefore in this sense I think she tends to be rather short-sighted. Tomorrow's papers and what's going to happen next week is absolutely overwhelmingly important to her, and the more distant trends and the really fundamental changes that are going on in the world and perhaps in the country are things that she thinks about less. Any person can only be themselves and they each have their talents, and hers are very very noticeable, but I don't think they include a profoundness or depth or far-sightedness.

Jim Prior also thinks a bit more breadth would be in order:

Prior:

She was always a great one for her boxes and I think she spent too much time dealing with the detail and never enough time looking at the long-term aspects. I must say I think she dealt with the housekeepng very well indeed. But I don't think that, at that time at any rate, and I think probably even now, she ever really spent enough time on the broad visionary picture, which is what a prime minister and a statesman of her quality and her reputation should be doing.

In trying to sort out the truth about this, there are several layers to be uncovered. Let's start at the global level. It is often said that Mrs Thatcher has been the instrument of a world-wide phenomenon, the British expression of some profound international shift of ideas away from the collectivist consensus towards individualism and other shibboleths beloved of the right. Mrs Thatcher's closest co-religionist in this reassertion of the faith is President Reagan. When we asked the President whether he thought their shared fulfilment of its precepts will have shifted the pendulum permanently, he was optimistic:

Reagan:
I have to believe that it will, because I think both of our countries had gone through a period in which, in some ways, we lost faith in our own people, and we began to turn back to government doing everything and government being looked to for things that properly belonged with the people and with the private sector. And I think there has been a recognition of that. I haven't been calling it Conservatism so much any more as commonsense, and yes, I think we have made a turn, and that it will be a long time, and I hope never, before people see themselves reverting to this statism and this belief that government must take over and do everything.

But considered worldwide, this is not wholly convincing. It is perfectly true that world economic recession has imposed remarkably similar economic policies on a wide variety of governments. But as the former West German Chancellor Helmut Schmidt says, the concept of global Thatcherism – much though the British Treasury likes to perceive its instructive presence in many corners from east to west – is an inadequate explanation of the observable political facts:

Schmidt:
In Italy and France you have the opposite – Socialist prime minister in Italy, Socialist president in France. No, it was not a trend towards the right. In Europe it was a trend to change governments because former governments obviously could not deal with the economic questions in a sufficient way. If you had a Conservative government in place then you wanted a Socialist government. If you had a Socialist government or a Labour government or a Social Democratic government in place you wanted a Conservative one. I was the last one to be cut off under this very understandable natural reaction of the national electorates.[1] In America it is quite a different thing; the

---

[1] On 6 March 1983 in the West German election, the coalition led by the Christian Democrat Helmut Kohl won a majority of 85 seats over Helmut Schmidt's S.P.D.

change from Ford to Carter and again from Carter to Reagan had absolutely different psychological and domestic political components from those which affected the changes of government in Europe. No, there is no general turn to the right, and there won't be a general turn to the left and there is no general mood of public opinion in Europe so far.

Nor, coming closer to home, should one be too impressed by the repeated assertion that Mrs Thatcher has, of herself, changed the intellectual climate in Britain in some unprecedented way. This is often spoken of as being akin to one of the seven labours of Hercules, successfully accomplished. Roy Jenkins puts it in a salutary context:

Jenkins:
Mind you, I think if anyone has been the leader of a major party for a long time and has exercised power for a substantial proportion of that period – and she's been leader for ten years now and prime minister for six years – I think almost anybody who has done that, whether they be good or bad, changes the intellectual climate. I think Baldwin changed the intellectual climate. I think to some extent Neville Chamberlain changed the intellectual climate. I think Attlee changed the intellectual climate. I think Macmillan changed the intellectual climate. It's very difficult to think of anybody who's been leader of a party and prime minister for such a period, who at the end of it hasn't left a slightly different intellectual climate from what they began with. So that in itself is not necessarily a tribute.

He's not saying, of course, that there's been no change. But what sort of change has it been? How large is its scope? How long will it last? One very senior former civil servant who worked closely with her, without ever being a natural sympathiser, once said that her most lasting single contribution will have been to remove the flannel from the habitual mental processes of government. Surely David Howell is right when he, too, identifies this as one sharp quality which does identify her around the world:

Howell:
Mrs Thatcher does stand for something all round the globe. I mean in America she's regarded very favourably indeed as a real force fitting into a modern world which is not a collectivised, centralised world. It's something different, not exactly a world of individualism, I think it's more a world like the one de Tocqueville described,[1] of small associations of people rather

---

[1] Alexis de Tocqueville, *De la Démocratie en Amérique* (1835).

than giant governments and giant trade unions. I also think she's admired all over the world because in a sea of bureaucratic waffle and delay and official duplicity she appears to be able, or anyway to want, to chop through all that. So she's the anti-bureaucrat in an age of bureaucracy.

Or, rather paradoxically, the supreme governor who does not believe in government! That was certainly one of the stylistic revolutions she proposed. And she's begun to accomplish it. The number of civil servants has been cut from 732,000 to 599,000, an 18% drop.[1] Bureaucracy in business has been cut by privatising public sector industries. The number of local authorities is being reduced. The anti-bureaucrat lives, even after six years at the seductive centre of the bureaucratic machine.

Another revolution was at least implied by her becoming Prime Minister at all. Could the cause of feminism have taken a more impregnable citadel? Throughout our inquiry a lot of witnesses, almost all men, have talked about the difference her gender makes to her style and personal relations. But what about policy? Wouldn't her arrival have a momentous effect on the balance of the sexes throughout British society? Here the record is a nullity, mainly, as Neil Kinnock is shrewd enough to see, because she has no serious interest in the matter:

Kinnock:

I don't think she's ever felt any sense of sexual inferiority and that's to her great credit. My criticism may be that she hasn't exploited the fact of being a woman prime minister in the cause of the advancement of womankind to the degree which she could have. In these six years that she has been Prime Minister there are no tangible ways in which she's deliberately sought to assist the advancement of over half our population. Whether we are talking about wages and the attitude to wages, or talking about access to university or we're talking about access to the medical profession or we're talking about the esteem offered towards women in general and the opportunities offered to them in general, Mrs Thatcher has either taken affairs in a retrograde direction or done nothing positive in order to try and improve the lot of womankind on the basis of merit and on the basis of justice to ensure that they get a fair crack of the whip.

All of which has been the gravest disappointment to Barbara

---

[1] *Civil Service Statistics*, 1985.

Castle. Originally, as is clear from the diary entries she wrote when Mrs Thatcher became leader of the Tory party, Mrs Castle was tremendously enthusiastic about this sudden appearance of a woman who exceeded even her own successful ascent into the topmost ranks of politics:[1]

Castle:

I believed instinctively, I suppose, that she'd be a womanly woman, whereas of course, she hasn't been a woman's woman at all. She's been someone for herself and has shown almost a contempt for her own sex in the way she has used her power as prime minister. Of course she has sex consciousness, I mean she wouldn't bother so much about her appearance, her grooming, the projection of herself in a favourable physical light all the time, if she weren't sexually conscious. But that's different from what I mean. Her treatment of the services that matter so much to women, that liberate them from domestic servitudes, all the social services, has shown that she's had no compassion at all for the working woman struggling to deal with a home, earn a wage, deal with an elderly parent, perhaps a mentally handicapped child, sickness in the family. These services don't arouse her interest at all.

So what has she been interested in? In Chapter Four her former economic adviser Sir Alan Walters looked backwards to the Victorian society she has sometimes idealised.[2] But does she have a big picture of the future, and what are its components? If vision there be, who else will put it into words? Sir Geoffrey Howe?

Howe:

She does have a vision of the future. A vision of a more prosperous future. A future in which people have got a greater command over their own lives. A more peaceful future. And she cares passionately about those things, I think.

Not perhaps the most compelling description. But can we find a better one? No doubt it's only an accident, but it is not entirely insignificant that this comes from a Labour politican. Maybe the critical eye clears the mind. But in Michael Meacher's case it enables him to say succinctly what Thatcherism has really been all about, and also permits him to see pluses as well as minuses,

---

[1] Barbara Castle, Labour MP 1945–79, was Minister of Transport 1965–8, Secretary of State for Employment and Productivity 1968–70, and Secretary of State for Social Services 1974–6.

[2] See page 85.

Thatcherite values that may now be shared as well as those which he roundly rejects:

Meacher:

The concern for value for money, for greater efficiency, for the view that you can't expect a job for life, that there are penalties to competitiveness, that higher standards are needed, that genuine commitment and hard work is a virtue – all of that is something she emphasises and I would agree with it. The trouble is it is linked with a system of values in which the rich are cosseted and the poor are penalised; in which competitiveness is exhorted without any regard for the losers, and the price of competition is that there are bound to be losers, however meritorious they are; and a total lack of concern for those who lack some of the capabilities or social opportunities of some of their peers; and a total disregard for – indeed an intensification of – the injustices of the class system.

A natural Labour reaction. But what Mr Meacher said at the beginning of that assessment does point to the possibility of a new kind of synthesis even on the left, incorporating at least some of the specific elements mentioned by the former Tory party Chairman, Cecil Parkinson, when we asked him, off the cuff, to enumerate some of the particulars:

Parkinson:

Take the theme of nationalisation. She believes that having lost forty thousand million pounds in the nationalised industries, the experiment is a failure, and that one shouldn't learn to live with it, one should actually change that circumstance. We have a very determined privatisation programme. There has been the most tremendous push by this government to spread ownership of companies, control of jobs, self employment and so on, sales of council houses is the most obvious one, tax policy is another one – there's been a very substantial reduction in the rates of tax and an attempt to try to tackle the tax problem at the bottom end. It isn't a series of incidental activities. They're all part of a tremendous push to give people more control over various aspects of their own lives and to make them less dependent on the politicians and the bureaucrats. And I think she has this very clear vision of the sort of society she wants.

As we now see, at least one thing on that list, council house sales, once anathema to Labour politicians, has been quietly admitted to the Labour party programme. In fact, the whole concept of the state as warder, as controller, as restrainer of enterprise is one which leading Labour politicians, in deference surely to Thatcherism's more popular aspects, are trying to shake off.

But is this really a grand vision? Or is it more like painting-by-numbers: a portrait of society put together in colours whose arrangement is stiffly ordered by the statistics of material wealth, mediated only by the immutable figuring of the public sector borrowing requirement? Jim Prior is one Conservative who, after six years of Thatcherism, is still not sure what it adds up to:

Prior:

I'm not certain it does add up to a vision. I think it's much more an aspiration than a vision. I think a vision is rather more than that. A vision is how you see a society as a whole, what sort of society you want to create in Britain, what impact that has on the rest of the world and what impact Britain has on Europe and so on. I don't believe that enabling people to own their own shares and own their own house, however desirable those things are, is in fact a visionary concept of what a society ought to be. It's more than that. I think those are very helpful things and things I would always support, but they're not to me as important as understanding the patriotism and the ideals of people.

The people who must be encompassed by the vision, moreover, include a lot who do not easily fit the picture of a society taking off, unshackled, to the stars.

Prior:

I think that one has to understand that there are only a small number of people in Britain at any one time who aspire to greatness. You can be just as great a patriot, have just as great ideals for your family, whether you happen to be a very successful person or whether you're doing a comparatively mundane job. And I think that one of the problems that the Conservative party doesn't seem to realise at the moment is that most of us are very ordinary people, and we don't aspire to greatness, and sometimes the tendency is to think that everyone ought to aspire to greatness and when they don't succeed in aspiring to greatness that they've somehow let the side down. Now that isn't what I think Britain is about.

But is it what Thatcherism is about? Failures not wanted on voyage. Away with compassion, up with success. Hers has been a government which, at least through its first term and into the beginning of its second, followed an unusual course.

Lord Boyd-Carpenter, who served in the Conservative governments led by Churchill, Eden, Macmillan and Home, puts it
simply:

Boyd-Carpenter:

Her government is the first Conservative government for a
very long time, perhaps since the time of Disraeli, that has
really sought not merely to talk Conservative policies but to
put them into effect.

Chris Patten, MP, was Director of the Conservative Research
Department when it all began:[1]

Patten:

She's the only party leader I can think of, certainly in the post-
war period, who's been more radical in government than in
opposition. As you know the normal feature is exactly the
reverse. I have to admit that I was surprised by the energy and
dash and radicalism of Mrs Thatcher after 1979. I think in some
ways she's been more radical, though running up against con-
straints, not the least of which is what our traditional supporters are prepared to tolerate. That's the most difficult
constraint of all for her, I think.

This is a point which stands close to her present dilemmas, and is
highly germane to the question of what history's verdict will be.
Remember what these traditional supporters have now shown
they won't tolerate? In 1984, the Education Department got as far
as announcing plans to cut student grants; Tory backbench
pressure compelled its withdrawal. In 1985 strong pre-budget
rumours prepared the way for a cut in the tax relief on mortgage
interest, and also for a new tax on pension funds. Both proposals
were stillborn, again because of party feeling. Yet these were
supposed to be keys to the next stage of the Thatcher revolution:
further cuts in public spending, further openings for cuts in
income tax. Radicals who want this, who enormously approve of
her direction and disagree with what Jim Prior was saying just
now, have been disappointed. They think the party has held the
Prime Minister back. In Chapter 3 Peter Walker, the celebrated
wet, said the performance had been better than the rhetoric,
thank goodness.[2] A well-known dry radical, Lord Harris of High
Cross, of the Institute of Economic Affairs, wishes the rhetoric
had been fulfilled:

---

[1] 1966–70.
[2] Page 69.

Harris:
Certainly the rhetoric is radical, and highly satisfactory, but on issue after issue I am disappointed with the progress of the government, and I think that she could quite reasonably blame her colleagues for that. She wouldn't necessarily want to blame them in public, but she can say that she's held back by the conservative element in the Tory party, because in my view she is the liberal element.

If this is the correct analysis, then she's probably gone as far as she can go. If all that holds her back is the party, and not some deeper, less exclusive force, then one must reply by saying that she's got the party by now about as close to her own image as it is ever likely to be. Peter Shore, watching from the Labour side, offers an analysis which many factions would agree with:

Shore:
Those who used to be on the extreme edges of the Conservative party are now in the centre of the Conservative party and that's very important. She's brought about a transformation in her own party, not complete, but we know how great it has been. When you look at her Cabinet today, and compare it with the one that she assembled in 1979 you can see the difference. But outside the Tory party has she really changed the national picture and aspirations, how people see their country and see themselves? That I doubt very much. She wins arguments, she defeats opponents, but she doesn't convince them.

Here surely Peter Shore has hit on a critical truth about the Thatcher phenomenon. It has captured power in the Tory party. It has changed the direction of economic policy. It's had big effects on the intellectual climate. It got a thumping majority in the 1983 election. It has also ridden with great aplomb a long series of lucky breaks: Labour's collapse into extremism, the split on the left, the adventitious benefits conferred by General Galtieri[1] and the British fighting man. Luck has indeed played an uncommon part in Mrs Thatcher's success. But has she really convinced the country of her vision? Do people understand it? Can she persuade them to follow her still further down the tunnel towards the light that may not be there?

This problem of securing consent has finally begun to trouble some of those who originally thought, with her, that consensus

---

[1] General Galtieri, President of Argentina December 1981–June 1982, when Argentina invaded the Falkland Islands in April 1982.

was the bane of Britain. Sir John Hoskyns, once her policy adviser in No. 10, was one of her strongest ideological props. For him, consensus meant fudging, presided over by the civil service. Now, having left government, he seems to have learned that securing assent is an absolute political imperative, especially when you're trying to change the nation:

Hoskyns:
What I've always felt tends to get left out in these calculations is the political strategy. How do you persuade enough people that it is in the general interest even where sometimes there will be losers? This business of explaining the size of the problem, explaining the awful consequences of doing nothing, and then winning that dreaded word, a consensus, as humanely and carefully and sensibly as possible – grappling with the nettles – that does take time. I would have guessed that it could take the rest of this parliament to set the stage for what they might do if they won a third term.

Lord Harris, who earlier was expressing disappointment with the progress of this government, dislikes talk of waiting for the third term:

Harris:
I've been a bit discomforted by the way that Conservatives who used to talk about the second term as being the great period when radical changes would be fully brought forward, when I speak to them now, say they look forward to the third term. It is very much more difficult to unravel a lot of these programmes, particularly in taxation and welfare, than was ever contemplated back in the hopeful days of 1979.

Welfare reform has indeed proved an almost invincibly complex problem. But even in a third term, it would continue to be a test of whether the country and the government can survive Mrs Thatcher's appetite for high-risk politics: the very thing Barbara Castle admires her for:

Castle:
I think we've got a couple of things we could learn from Margaret Thatcher – one is to have a courage and a fire not to change course just because the flak is flying. That doesn't mean that one has to go to the Iron Lady extremes that she has gone to, because she didn't listen to people in the first place anyhow. But if you have listened to people and you've decided this is what you must do, you should stick to it. And the second thing we should learn from Margaret Thatcher is that

the best form of defence is always attack and she's brought that to a brilliant political art. I remember in the last election the weaker her case was the more she counter attacked, and it's all part of this giving of the impression that one knows where one wants to go and has the courage to face the risks of trying to get there.

One great trophy of this willingness to attack was the head of the miners' leader, Arthur Scargill. The triumph over the NUM, who had to return to work in March 1985 without a settlement after a year-long strike that divided the Union, has probably marked politics permanently; it's certainly changed an important balance of power. But the lust for battle does not impress Neil Kinnock. He sees a different sort of response to the years of Thatcherism. The 1980s have seen the eclipse of moderate or 'wet' conservatism, and a rise in the outspokenness of non-political persons such as bishops and even judges, making more or less coded attacks on Thatcherism. To Mr Kinnock this foreshadows the essential impermanence of Thatcherite methods. These will be a reaction against the style, even though she has, as he admits, shifted the argument to the right:

Kinnock:

Yes, but in the process of doing that, of course, she's given a renaissance to the consensus. What we've been seeing in the last eighteen months or so – something which I always thought was inevitable, the question was when it would happen – is a rediscovery not only of the pale pink Toryism, but a re-examination by a lot of people of their values. This is one of the reasons that we see the church to some extent in conflict in the assertion of its values with the values that are espoused by Mrs Thatcher. So, yes, the political context has changed, and the basic British political context of patience, of tolerance, of compassion, not soft options at all, in fact very tough virtues in British politics, are now being reasserted because of the shock to the system that came as a consequence of Mrs Thatcher's particular form of brutal approach. I don't think there's a fairer phrase that can be applied.

How great this shock has been, and how permanently it has rearranged the landscape, are the questions the historian will address. Even on an interim basis, taking this arbitrary moment in time as one for a speculative judgement, they are not easy to answer. Such clarity of profile evokes no equal clarity of verdict. At one extreme stands the opinion of a civil servant. Is Sir

Douglas Wass, formerly Permanent Secretary at the Treasury, engaged here in a classic piece of mandarin's wish-fulfilment, or will this really be seen as a more centrist time than most people are now aware?

Wass:

My own idiosyncratic view is that she will be seen more in the mainstream of British politics than a lot of people think and perhaps even she thinks. In many ways I'm struck by the similarities of this government in basic essentials with its predecessors. In other words, I think there is less of a change than many people think. The prime minister, for instance, although clearly what many people call a conviction politician, is of course at the same time a politician, and she knows that concessions have to be made, that compromises have to be struck, and they are continually being struck in the ongoing political process. The rhetoric in fact, the declarations of intent, are rather different from what has been possible to achieve, and I think history may see it more in terms of what was achieved than what was declared.

But if this turns out to be right, if the achievement doesn't match the declared ambition, Chris Patten is sure she'll think she's failed:

Patten:

Her most distinguishing mark is a sort of Shavian belief in the ability of people to change events.[1] She followed a prime minister, I think rather a good prime minister, Jim Callaghan, who took the view, rightly or wrongly, that the best anybody could do was to manage the decline of Britain in as humane and caring a fashion as possible. Now that strategy fell to pieces in the winter of 1978-9. Mrs Thatcher took over committed to a very different view: that what governing Britain had to be about was arresting and reversing the decline which had been going on for either twenty or fifty or a hundred years – it depends who you read. And that was clearly what she perceived as her mission. I think she will be happy to be judged by whether or not she manages to achieve that.

In one respect, says David Howell, she already has. We've heard a lot of well-judged criticism of Mrs Thatcher from Mr Howell in earlier chapters, but on this point he is positive; that the belief in the possibility of recovery has been reborn:

---

[1] See page 46n.

Howell:

There was a feeling in the '70s, and I certainly shared it, that we'd got bogged down in a sort of defeatism that the trade unions were huge, powerful, unbeatable, unreasonable, but nevertheless they had to be compromised with, there had to be some kind of appeasement and that the best you could do was hold the line for a while and then things would move on their way. And you can remember pundits writing books entitled 'The Future that Doesn't Work' and gloomy things like that. Now, I think that attitude has gone. That defeatism of the '60s and '70s, the feeling that we were always going to be passengers, always going to be laggards, we couldn't compete with our neighbours let alone with Asia. I think that has gone.

But this is by no means enough. We may now believe in the possibility of competing with Japan and South Korea. But this just may be a delusion. The figures are not encouraging.[1] Besides, rather more than the ending of union appeasement is needed as evidence to prove that the assault on Keynesian economics has worked. In a broader sense, has Mrs Thatcher been a truly national leader? In response to this question, Lord Whitelaw, her faithful deputy, did not trot out a party platitude:

Whitelaw:

At moments I think she is a truly national leader. I think, for example, in the handling of the Falklands, she expressed a very wide opinion throughout the nation, and was widely supported. That's why I think that on some big issues she does become a national leader. I think on smaller issues no one can ever command a very widespread consensus because probably on so many issues that come before us there is no such thing.

Certainly there has been no such thing in the last six years. The old consensus on matters small and large has been destroyed. A new one has yet to be built, its construction impeded by Mrs Thatcher's continuing aversion to the very idea, wherever on the spectrum it gathers. The legacy of division features quite large in Jim Prior's reckoning of the balance sheet:

---

[1] In 1984 the figures taken from the worldwide sales of the thirteen top motor manufacturers were: Japan £2,768,000; UK £1,273,000. *Data Research Institute International Automotive Services.*

In September 1984 the UK had a merchant shipping order book of 456,775 tons; South Korea 5,000,000 tons and Japan 13,510,000 tons. *Lloyd's Register of Shipping 1985.*

Prior:

I've no doubt she's going to leave a permanent mark on this country. I think that she will go down with a great deal of credit as someone who restored stability to Britain after a pretty shaky period. I think we will have found that the early eighties have got a much better balance between management and unions than we've had before. I think all that is to her credit. I think that perhaps the long-term view on her may not be as favourable as people's views are now, in that I think she's missed some opportunities in Europe which I think are important, and I think that the country is more divided now than it was, and I think there is a penalty to be paid for all that. She isn't a One-Nation Conservative. She isn't really a believer in the 1944 White Paper on Employment.[1] And I just feel that the country has lost quite a bit of cohesion in the last few years which will not redound to her credit, but I've no doubt that the pluses will far outweigh the minuses and if we hadn't had this strong lady, this first woman prime minister in 1979, we might be in a hell of a lot bigger mess than we're in.

That depends which part of the mess you're talking about. Many people in many corners of the economy, whether they're bosses or workers, would think the mess they find themselves in could not be more intolerable. Have they had enough? Have we all had enough? Will the Tory party find, when Margaret Thatcher submits herself to the people for a third time, that a combination of boredom, impatience and fatigue – three afflictions, only one of which she personally experiences – drives the people to throw her out? What this will depend on is whether they agree with her analysis, and in particular her reigning conviction that the past – all time before her – must be obliterated. Roy Jenkins, a nodal figure from that era, is well placed to assess the nature of the break:

Jenkins:

Whether Mrs Thatcher will have made a great break with the past, I don't know, but what's beyond that is the question whether it was desirable to make a great break with the past. Before Mrs Thatcher says that she broke away from all this softness, weakness, degradation which followed from Macmillan, from Heath, from Wilson obviously, from Callaghan, I think she really has to show how she has made the country better

---

[1] *Employment Policy 1944 (Cmnd 6527).*

than it was in what she regards as the bad old days. And let's not do it in party terms, let's do it in Conservative party terms. I mean how exactly is Britain functioning economically or politically better today than it was at the peak of the Macmillan period in 1960? Unemployment is clearly vastly higher. Inflation is still higher. The pound doesn't look exactly stronger than it did then. The rate of investment, the rate of growth is lower.[1] What I object to about the view that by breaking with the past somehow you've achieved some great magnificence for the future, is that it's totally irrational. It's based on a theory of economics which is based on valour and not on achievement and I think this is extremely dangerous. There are some fields in which valour's a great thing, but management of the economy is not one of them. Management of the economy is an economic material process designed to achieve material ends and ought to be judged on whether it achieves them or not.

Whether it will achieve them is the question which remains to be decided. But we may be quite certain that Margaret Thatcher will not give up the struggle. What we have established through the testimony of many intimate witnesses is the crucial importance of her personality to what her government does. Her politics proceeds from her character. Her style of leadership turns heavily on her being a woman. Her economics may be drawn from other men's ideas, but it is she who has held them together and taken the political consequences. She still thinks she has a nation to save. No one else can do the job of scorching socialism off the face of Britain. Whether people want this is almost beside the point. Whether they love her for it is even less relevant. This is her time, dominated by her character. To her credit, she will never have an alibi. If we perceive a triumph, she will take the palm. If, on the other hand, we never do emerge into the sunlight at the end of that famous tunnel, she has ensured that there is nobody else to take the blame.

---

[1]

	1960	1985
Unemployment	392,800	3,240,900
Dollars to the £	$2.8	$1.29
Inflation	1.1%	6.9%
Rate of investment	9.7%	7.7%
Rate of growth	5.5%	3.1%

Index

Kinnock, Neil, 10, 76; on her as a woman, 39, 82, 131; on her House of Commons performance, 53; on cleverness, 63; on her economic philosophy, 75; on compassion, 84; on political virility, 91; on foreign policy, 109, 120; on US relations, 110–11; on patriotism, 116; on consensus, 138

law and order, her attitude to, 87
Lewin, Lord, 10, 118–19
Liverpool, Lord, 121

Machel, President Samora, 100
Macleod, Iain, 26
Macmillan, Harold, 23, 52, 130, 135, 141, 142
Mao Tse-tung, 122
Meacher, Michael, 10; on her as a communicator, 68; on her image, 79; comparison with Mao Tse-tung, 122; on Thatcherite values, 132–3
Methodism, 15, 19
Middleton, Sir Peter, 51
'milk-snatcher', 26–7
Mitterrand, President François, 100, 112, 115

Nairne, Sir Patrick, 10, 49, 50
Neave, Airey, 30, 31, 36
Newman, Bernard, 14
Northern Ireland, 31, 80, 96
NUM, 74, 79n, 138

Observer, the, 16
Open University, 26
Oppenheim, Sally, 10, 21
Oxford University, her time at, vi, 13, 16, 18, 36
Oxford University Conservative Association, 17, 18

Parkinson, Cecil, 10, 31, 88; on her as a woman, 38; on 'one of us', 54; on her guile, 94; on Thatcherism, 133
Parsons, Sir Anthony, 10, 51, 101; on her inexperience, 98; on her diplomatic style, 100, 101; on Rhodesia settlement, 102–3; on Soviet Union, 106; on US relations, 110; on her vision, 128
Patten, Chris, 10, 33; on her dominance, 46; on intellectual influence, 75–6; on radicalism, 135; on her historic place, 139
Pensions and National Insurance, vi, 23
Pile, Sir William, 10, 22, 40, 59; on her character, 12–13, 25, 48; on her as Education Secretary, 24–5; on her ambition, 33–4; on wisdom, 62–3; on her honesty, 93
Ponting, Clive, 93
Prentice, Reg, 10, 37, 45–6, 81, 126
Prior, Jim, 10, 32n, 40, 47–8; on her as Education Secretary, 27; on Sir Keith Joseph, 29; on leadership contest, 30; on Cabinet style, 42–3; on her attitude to unions, 72–3; on economic policy, 76; on loyalty, 96; on vision, 128, 134; on her historic place, 140–1
privatisation, 74–5, 133
public expenditure, her attitude to, 27–8, 54

Pym, Francis, 10, 34; on Cabinet style, 43; on Conservative party, 54–5; on her vision, 59, 128; on economic policy, 77–8; on her inexperience, 98–9; on her diplomatic style, 99, 101; on Rhodesia settlement, 103; on EEC budget, 114

race, her attitude to, 87
Reagan, President Ronald, 11, 100, 111–12, 130; on Williamsburg summit, 20; on her as a woman, 35; on his relations with her, 107–11; on Falklands War, 116; on Conservatism, 129
Rhodesia (Zimbabwe), 102–4
riots, her attitude to, 86–7
Roberts, Alfred, 13, 15, 16, 21
Roberts, Mrs Beatrice, 16

Saatchi and Saatchi, 94
St Francis, 79, 80, 96
St John Stevas, Norman, 43
Scargill, Arthur, 79, 88, 138
Schmidt, Helmut, 11, 99, 111, 115, 129–30
Sherman, Sir Alfred, 11, 29, 30, 47, 60
Shore, Peter, 11; on 'one of us', 53–4; on her economic philosophy, 58, 72, 74, 77; on her as a communicator, 63–4; on class, 88–9; on the Conservative party, 136
Siberian pipeline, 109
Soames, Lord, 103–4
Somerville College, 17, 20
Soviet Union, her attitude to, 104–7, 117
Star Wars, 110
Steel, David, 11, 52, 86–7, 103–4

Talking Politics, 18n
Tebbit, Norman, 11, 74, 77, 122n, 125; on entrepreneurs, 70; on patronage, 71; on wealth-creation, 83–4
Thatcher, Denis, 21, 22
trade unions, her attitude to, 72–4
Treasury, vi, 20, 27, 66

unemployment, her attitude to, 65, 74, 76, 115
USA, her relations with, 107–12

Vaughan, Dame Janet, 11, 17, 20, 36

Walker, Peter, 11, 69, 135
Walters, Sir Alan, 11, 29, 44, 67, 124, 132; on her instincts, 62; on the 1981 budget, 65–6; on Victorian values, 84–5
Wass, Sir Douglas, 11, 20–1, 27, 51n; on Cabinet style, 46–7; on her economic philosophy, 61–2; on her historic place, 138–9
Whitelaw, Lord, 11, 32n, 33, 41, 43, 86; on leadership contest, 32; on her as a woman, 39–40; on her vulnerability, 81; on being in touch, 90–1; on guile, 93–4; on Falklands War, 117–18; on leadership, 140
Wickstead, Margaret, 11, 13–14, 16, 18, 19, 36, 92–3
Wilson, Harold, 37, 47, 77, 141
World in Action, 87n
Wyatt, Sir Woodrow, 73